The Expert at the Card Table

THE CLASSIC TREATISE ON CARD MANIPULATION

S. W. ERDNASE

ILLUSTRATED BY M. D. SMITH
WITH A NEW FOREWORD BY
MARTIN GARDNER

To Adam from Grandma & Grandpa

DOVER PUBLICATIONS, INC.
NEW YORK

Bibliographical Note

This Dover edition, first published in 1995, is an unabridged republication of the work originally published by the author in 1902 under the title *Artifice, Ruse and Subterfuge at the Card Table: A Treatise on the Science and Art of Manipulating Cards.* The binding of the original bears the title *The Expert at the Card Table,* by which the work is now generally known. A new foreword has been written specially for the Dover edition by Martin Gardner.

International Standard Book Number: 0-486-28597-9

Manufactured in the United States of America
Dover Publications, Inc., 31 East 2nd Street, Mineola, N.Y. 11501

CONTENTS

FOREWORD TO THE DOVER EDITION

The Expert at the Card Table, with the cryptic name of S. W. Erdnase on its title page, is the most famous, the most carefully studied book ever published on the art of manipulating cards at gaming tables. Books had been written previously about card cheating, but none went into such technical detail or contained so many trade secrets never before revealed.

Magicians treasure *The Expert at the Card Table* because its "sleights" — false cuts, false shuffles, second deals, bottom deals and so on — are as essential to a card conjuror as they are to crooked gamblers. The author was almost as interested in card magic as in gambling methods. Originally, he intended his book to deal only with gambling techniques, but he was persuaded to add a section on magic to make the book more salable.

In 1994 Ricky Jay was hugely successful in Manhattan with his one-man magic show featuring card magic. A highlight of his performance was a presentation of the classic four-ace trick described by the author in terms of queens instead of aces. When I saw Ricky demonstrate this trick on television, a few years before he opened his New York show, I was astounded to learn that the "patter" he used was taken word for word from the Erdnase book.

Although the first edition of 1902 had slim sales, mainly through magic shops, the book gradually became recognized as *the* classic treatise on how to cheat at card games. It has never been out of print. Dai Vernon, one of the great creative card magicians of this century, knew the book by heart. He even annotated an edition, titled *Revelations*, in 1984. A more elaborate commentary, *The Annotated Erdnase*, by Darwin Ortiz, appeared in 1991.

Who was S. W. Erdnase? Early on it was noticed that when this name is spelled backward it becomes E. S. Andrews. Half a century ago I was instrumental in tracking down the author's true identity. He was Milton Franklin Andrews, a native of Hartford, Connecticut, who left home as a youth to become one of the nation's most successful card swindlers. A man with a violent temper and a fondness for prostitutes, he was wanted by the police as a prime suspect in the murder of Bessie Bouton, one of his many girl friends, in Cold Springs, Colorado.

In 1905, when the San Francisco police finally located Andrews and broke into his apartment, he shot himself and the woman then living with him. He was 33. (The sordid details of Andrews' character and ignoble life are covered thoroughly in *The Man Who Was Erdnase*, a book on which Jeff Busby and I assisted the author, Bart Whaley. It was published in 1991 by Busby, who owns a magic-supply house in Wallace, Idaho. Whaley's richly illustrated and carefully documented biography also discusses many recent improvements on Andrews' methods.)

Although there no longer is any doubt that Milton Andrews was the author of *The Expert at the Card Table*, a great mystery still remains. Andrews never went to college, and a lengthy letter he sent to the *San Francisco Examiner*, offering to surrender to the police if they would meet certain conditions, makes clear that he could not have achieved the polished prose in which this book is written. Who, then, was the book's skillful editor?

We know that Andrews paid a Chicago printer to publish his book in 1902. We also know that he paid a Chicago artist, Marshall D. Smith, to illustrate the book. I had the pleasure of locating the elderly Smith when he still lived in Chicago. He told me how, as a young man, he had gone to Andrews' hotel room on a cold winter day to make pencil sketches of the gambler's hands as he held the cards above a felt-covered board that you see in some of the drawings. But who did Andrews pay to edit his manuscript? To this day the question remains unanswered. In *The Man Who Was Erdnase*, Whaley gives excellent reasons for thinking it was William John Hilliar, an English magician who settled in America and who ghosted books by magicians T. Nelson Downs and Howard Thurston.

Whether Andrews actually killed Bessie Bouton we shall never know. It is possible he was no more than a likely suspect. There is no doubt, however, that his short life was dangerous and tormented. He must have known that his book would be his only claim to undying fame. He was immensely proud of his skills and his original contributions to card work and, as he tells in his book, was frustrated by the necessity of keeping his talents hidden. Surely that was why he concealed his last name in so simple a way that it would be easy to discover.

There is controversy over how much material Andrews omitted — secrets he preferred not to reveal — as well as the extent to which he may have knowingly given inferior methods. In some cases Smith's drawings are misleading. For instance, the illustration for the slip cut (Figure 11) shows how *not* to perform this valuable move. The text itself does not support the picture. Nor does the text describe the best technique. As all card magicians should know, a slip cut is best made by pressing the index finger on the top card so that, when the bottom half of the deck is cut forward, the card slides with it to give the impression that the top half has been taken. Then the hand comes back to pick up the top half, which has not moved, and place it on the bottom half.

Much has been written in magic books and periodicals about Andrews' bottom deal. Almost all experts agree it is not the best technique. It is possible, I suppose, that Andrews may have practiced until he could deal undetectable bottoms by his method — or did he intentionally describe a technique he knew few readers could master? The same can be said of the bizarre "shifts" he invented.

In explaining how to deal seconds, Andrews again describes the more difficult method — one in which two cards are pushed over each time — but omits the easier method known today as "strike seconds."

We know that Andrews knew more than he gives in his book because in real life he was once caught cheating on a ship, while returning from Australia, by using what is called "the spread." Nowhere in his book is this maneuver described.

On page 19, after giving an excellent method for holding a bottom stock during a riffle shuffle, Andrews mentions two riffle shuffles that preserve a deck's entire order. They are known today as the "push through" and the "pull out" or "strip out" shuffle. Andrews gives two reasons for not explaining either shuffle: Each is "very difficult to perform perfectly," and "there is seldom a desire and never a necessity of preserving the complete order at a card table."

Here, then, is Andrews' masterpiece. No matter that some of his techniques have been improved over the years. Most of his methods are as useful today for magicians and card hustlers as they were in 1902. The book is still the bible of card "mechanics," and as much a delight to read as it was in the early years of this century.

MARTIN GARDNER

PREFACE

In offering this book to the public the writer uses no sophistry as an excuse for its existence. The hypocritical cant of reformed (?) gamblers, or whining, mealymouthed pretensions of piety, are not foisted as a justification for imparting the knowledge it contains. To all lovers of card games it should prove interesting, and as a basis of card entertainment it is practically inexhaustible. It may caution the unwary who are innocent of guile, and it may inspire the crafty by enlightenment on artifice. It may demonstrate to the tyro that he cannot beat a man at his own game, and it may enable the skilled in deception to take a postgraduate course in the highest and most artistic branches of his vocation. But it will not make the innocent vicious, or transform the pastime player into a professional; or make the fool wise, or curtail the annual crop of suckers; but whatever the result may be, if it sells it will accomplish the primary motive of the author, as he needs the money.

INTRODUCTION

The passion for play is probably as old, and will be as enduring, as the race of man. Some of us are too timid to risk a dollar, but the percentage of people in this feverish nation who would not enjoy winning one is very small. The passion culminates in the professional. He would rather play than eat. Winning is not his sole delight. Some one has remarked that there is but one pleasure in life greater than winning, that is, in making the hazard.

To be successful at play is as difficult as to succeed in any other pursuit. The laws of chance are as immutable as the laws of nature. Were all gamblers to depend on luck they would break about even in the end. The professional card player may enjoy the average luck, but it is difficult to find one who thinks he does, and it is indeed wonderful how mere chance will at times defeat the strongest combination of wit and skill. It is almost an axiom that a novice will win his first stake. A colored attendant of a "club-room," overhearing a discussion about running up two hands at poker, ventured the following interpolation: "Don't trouble 'bout no two han's, Boss. Get yo' own han'. De suckah, he'll get a han' all right, suah!" And many old players believe the same thing. However, the vagaries of luck, or chance, have impressed the professional card player with a certain knowledge that his more respected brother of the stock exchange possesses, viz. — manipulation is more profitable than speculation; so to make both ends meet, and incidentally a good living, he also performs his part with the shears when the lambs come to market.

Hazard at play carries sensations that once enjoyed are rarely forgotten. The winnings are known as "pretty money," and it is generally spent as freely as water. The average professional who is successful at his own game will, with the sublimest unconcern, stake his money on that of another's, though fully aware the odds are against him. He knows little of the real value of money, and as a rule is generous, careless and improvident. He loves the hazard rather than the stakes. As a matter of fact the principal difference between the professional gambler and the occasional gambler, is that the former is actuated by his love of the game and the latter by cupidity. A professional rarely "squeals" when he gets the worst of it; the man who has other means of livelihood is the hardest loser.

Advantages that are bound to ultimately give a percentage in favor of the professional are absolutely essential to his existence, and the means employed at the card table to obtain that result are thoroughly elucidated in this work. We have not been impelled to our task by the qualms of a guilty conscience, nor through the hope of reforming the world. Man cannot change his temperament, and few care to control it. While the passion for hazard exists it will find gratification. We have neither grievance against the fraternity nor sympathy for so-called "victims." A varied experience has impressed us with the belief that all men who play for any considerable stakes are looking for the best of it. We give the facts and conditions of our subject as we find them, though we sorrowfully admit that our own early knowledge was acquired at the usual excessive cost to the uninitiated.

When we speak of professional card players we do not refer to the proprietors or managers of gaming houses. The percentage in their favor is a known quantity, or can be readily calculated, and their profits are much the same as any business enterprise. Where the civil authorities countenance these institutions they are generally conducted by men of well known standing in the community. The card tables pay a percentage or "rake off," and the management provides a "look out" for the protection of its patrons. Where the gaming rooms must be conducted in secret the probabilities of the player's apparent chances being lessened are much greater. However, our purpose is to account for the unknown percentage that must needs be in favor of the professional card player to enable him to live.

There is a vast difference between the methods employed by the card conjurer in mystifying or amusing his audience; and those practiced at the card table by the professional, as in this case the entire conduct must be in perfect harmony with the usual procedure of the game. The slightest action that appears irregular, the least effort to distract attention, or the first unnatural movement, will create suspicion; and mere suspicion will deplete the company, as no one but a simon-pure fool will knowingly play against more than ordinary chances. There is one way by which absolute protection against unknown advantages may be assured, that is by never playing for money. But a perfect understanding of the risks that are taken may aid greatly in lessening the casualties. An intimate acquaintance with the modus operandi of card-table artifice does not necessarily enable one to detect the manipulation, but it certainly makes plain the chances to be guarded against, and with this cognition the mere suspicion of skill should at once induce symptoms of cold feet. This knowledge, or thorough comprehension of the possibilities of professional card playing, can be imparted only by practical illustration of the processes employed, and the reader desiring a complete understanding should take the deck in hand and work out for himself the action as it is described.

To discriminate and show clearly the two phases of card manipulation, the first part of this work is devoted to an exhaustive review of the many advantages that can be, have been, and are constantly taken at the card table, and to those particular methods of obtaining these advantages that are least liable to arouse suspicion. The exact manner in which each artifice is performed is fully described in minutia. Part second describes the sleights employed in conjuring and many very interesting card tricks.

CARD-TABLE ARTIFICE

Professional Secrets. — The secrets of professional card playing have been well preserved. Works on conjuring invariably devote much space to the consideration of card tricks, and many have been written exclusively for that purpose, yet we have been unable to find in the whole category more than an incidental reference to any card-table artifice; and in no instance are the principal feats even mentioned. Self-styled "ex-professionals" have regaled the public with astounding disclosures of their former wiles and wickedness, and have proven a wonderful knowledge of the subject by exhuming some antiquated moss-covered ruses as well known as nursery rhymes, and even these extraordinary revelations are calmly dismissed with the assertion that this or that artifice is employed; in nowise attempting to explain the process or give the detail of the action mentioned. If terrific denunciation of erstwhile associates, and a diatribe on the awful consequences of gambling are a criterion of ability, these purified prodigals must have been very dangerous companions at the card table.

Of course it is generally known that much deception is practiced at cards, but it is one thing to have that knowledge and quite another to obtain a perfect understanding of the methods employed, and the exact manner in which they are executed. Hence this work stands unique in the list of card books. We modestly claim originality for the particular manner of accomplishing many of the manœuvres described, and believe them vastly superior to others that have come under our observation. We do not claim to know it all. Many professionals have attained their success by improving old methods, or inventing new ones; and as certain artifices are first disclosed in this work so will others remain private property as long as the originators are so disposed.

We betray no confidences in publishing this book, having only ourselves to thank for what we know. Our tuition was received in the cold school of experience. We started in with the trusting nature of a fledgling, and a calm assurance born of overweening faith in our own potency. We bucked the tiger voluntarily, and censure no one for the inevitable result. A self-satisfied unlicked cub with a fairly fat bank roll was too good a thing to be passed up. We naturally began to imbibe wisdom in copious draughts at the customary sucker rates, but the jars to our pocketbook caused far less anguish than the heartrending jolts to our insufferable conceit. After the awakening our education progressed through close application and constant study of the game, and the sum of our present knowledge is proffered in this volume, for any purpose it may answer, to friend and foe, to the wise and the foolish, to the good and the bad, to all alike, with but one reservation, — that he has the price.

Hold Outs. — Many mechanical contrivances termed "hold outs" have been invented to aid the card player. The simplest form is a steel spring with an awl-like attachment at one end which can be pressed into the under side of almost any table in an instant. The spring snaps up against the table, the end curving slightly downwards to receive the cards. The thumb of either hand can put in or take several cards from the apparatus without the hands leaving the table.

A more complicated table machine passes the cards from below completely over the edge of the table, and the hands, held naturally on the table top, receive and make the discard without a sign to denote the procedure.

"Hold outs" that are adjusted to the person are of most ingenious construction and very expensive. A sleeve machine which passes the cards into and from the palm by spreading the knees may be worth from seventy-five dollars to several hundred dollars. Some are worked by arm pressure, some pass the cards through an opening in the vest about the usual height the hands are held. One of the most novel and perfect machines ever constructed makes the "sneak" by simply expanding the chest an inch or two, or taking a deeper breath than usual.

In almost all cases where "hold outs" are used the principal skill possessed by the player is that of working his apparatus perfectly and secreting the extra cards while in his hands; but to employ a machine successfully requires considerable address, and especially nerve. However, a full description of these devices or their uses is not contemplated by us. They can be purchased from the dealers in "club-room articles," and, anyway, the expert professional disdains their assistance. They are cumbersome, unnecessary, and a constant menace to his reputation.

Prepared Cards. — The subject of prepared cards is almost as foreign to the main purpose of this work as the preceding one of "hold outs," but a cursory review of the commoner kinds and their uses may not be out of place.

Marked cards, generally known as "readers," can be distinguished by the backs as readily as by the faces when the key is known. Printed cards are manufactured, but these are rarely used by professionals. The designs are not the same as those now of standard make, and consequently would be difficult to introduce. The usual plan is to mark the standard decks by hand. For the benefit of the unenlightened or curious reader we shall describe the process. It is not at all difficult, and a deck can be "doctored" in an hour or so.

Nearly all standard cards are red or blue. Marking inks absolutely indistinguishable from the printer's ink can be obtained from any of the dealers. Cards of intricate design are best adapted for the purpose. Each card is marked at both ends, so as to be read in any position. The peculiarity of the figures or design across the end is first closely considered, and twelve fairly distinct points, or dots or dashes, are noted and located. Then the four Aces are laid out, and with a fine pen the first point located is shortened barely enough to notice. The point is white and the background red or blue, the color of the ink used; and the slightest shortening of a single point or the obliteration of a single dot on a card, is undetectable unless it is known.

The four Aces are treated in this manner, then turned end for end, and the operation repeated. Then the Kings are doctored, the second point located being shortened in this instance. Then the four Queens at the third point, and so on throughout the deck for the twelve values; the absence of any mark denoting the Deuce. Now the suits are marked. Three additional points are located, possibly close to one corner. The first point marked say for Diamonds, the second for Clubs, third for Hearts and Spades left natural. Thus the operator at a glance, by noting the location of the two "blockouts," can instantly name the cards as they are dealt.

Combination systems lessen the number of points to be located. The design of the particular deck will suggest whether a dot, line, or blockout, would be least noticeable. It is seldom that two operators work alike. Cleverly done, it is almost impossible to detect, and unless suspicion is aroused quite so. Most of the supply houses keep a skilled operator constantly employed, and will mark any deck to order for about one dollar.

Some players make a practice of marking cards during the process of the game. The most desirable cards are creased or indented at certain locations as they happen to come into the player's possession, with the finger or thumb nail, which is kept pointed for the purpose; and in the course of an hour the principal cards can be readily distinguished. Another plan is to darken the edges with different prepared inks that are conveniently adjusted in pads. These manœuvres, while making nothing sure in a given instance, always net the operator a favorable percentage in the long run.

Prepared cards known as "Strippers" are much used by certain players. The desired cards are placed aside and the rest of the cards trimmed slightly along the sides; then the briefs are trimmed from nothing at middle of sides to the width of the cut deck at ends. This leaves a slight hump at sides of the desired cards when shuffled in the deck, and they can be drawn out at will and placed on top or bottom at option. The trimming is done with machines made for the purpose, and the cutting leaves the edges and the corners as smooth as glass.

There are many other methods of doctoring cards to meet the requirements of particular games, and the skill, or rather want of it, of the operator. By roughening the faces of some of the cards they will hold together, and are more easily retained while shuffling. Faro cards, used in connection with a certain form of "brace" box, are treated in this manner. In the construction of the various kinds of control boxes the acme of ingenuity and mechanical skill has been reached, and most extravagant prices are demanded and paid, for these innocent-appearing little silver-plated articles. Strippers may be used in Faro with little fear of detection, as the cards are never shuffled or cut by the players. A "crooked" box and a clever dealer can give the house a percentage that would impoverish a prince. Millions of dollars are wagered annually at Faro in this country. It is the most fascinating of layout games. However, we have reason to believe it is generally dealt on the square in gambling rooms that are run openly. The bank's percentage is satisfactory to the proprietors.

The "Cold Deck" is a pre-arranged pack that is introduced at an opportune moment. The cards are not marked, but two or more hands are set up ready for dealing. The name is probably derived from the fact that the deck must await its opportunity long enough to contract a chill in the interim. Little skill is required in making the exchange. It is almost invariably done quite openly, and in company where the attendants and players are in collusion. In most gaming rooms the decks are exchanged every hour or less. Sometimes the players will call for a new deck, but usually the exchange is made at the instance of the management. When the "cold deck" is sprung a "blind" shuffle is made by the dealer, a "blind" cut by an ally, and the hands fall in the desired order. Of course an exchange may be made by sleight-of-hand, but the player who can accomplish this feat successfully is generally well versed in the higher orders of card-table artifice, and will dispense with such makeshifts as "cold decks" or any kind of prepared cards.

Confederacy. — When two card experts work together their difficulties are greatly lessened. The opportunities of securing the desirable cards on the outset, that is before the shuffle, are doubled, and this is half the battle. If they understand each other perfectly they can often arrange one or two hands ready for dealing, and find little or no trouble at all in getting several desirable cards together while apparently gathering up the deck in the most careless manner. If sitting together so that one cuts on the other's deal the possibilities become so great that ordinary chances will be taken in perhaps nineteen deals out of twenty. Two or three coups in the course of an evening will not flush the quarry, and are quite sufficient to answer all purposes.

Advantages without dexterity can be taken in almost any card game when two or more players are in collusion, by the use of any secret code of signals that will disclose the hand of each to the others. For instance, in Poker the ally holding the best cards will be the only one to stay, thus playing the best hand of the allies against the rest; quite sufficient advantage to give a large percentage in favor of the combination. Again, the allies may resort to "crossfiring," by each raising until the other players drop out. There are hundreds of small but ultimately certain advantages to be gained in this manner, if collusion is not suspected. No single player can defeat a combination, even when the cards are not manipulated.

Two Methods of Shuffling. — As the reader obtains an understanding of the art of "advantage playing" it will be seen that the old-fashioned or hand shuffle gives the greater possibilities for running up hands, selecting desirable cards and palming. Many players never use the "riffle," that is shuffling on the table by springing the ends of two packets into each other, though this method is now by far the more prevalent among men who play for money. While the "riffle" cannot be employed for arranging the cards, save to a very limited extent, it is equally well adapted for retaining the top or bottom portion, or even the whole deck, in any prearranged order; and the "blind riffle" can be performed just as perfectly as the "blind" shuffle. A clever bottom dealer will usually employ the "riffle," as he rarely takes the trouble of running up a hand. His purpose in that respect is sufficiently answered by keeping the desired cards at the bottom. If he has an ally to "blind" cut, everything goes well, but if playing alone he must either palm the bottom cards for the cut or make a "shift" afterwards. The "shift" is very rarely attempted in any kind of knowing company, and it is awkward to make a palm when the "riffle" is used. The deck must be tilted on its side, and while the movement may pass as an effort at squaring up, it is not quite regular. The hand shuffle avoids the difficulty, as the deck is held naturally in easy position for palming, and not an instant is lost during the operation.

The hand shuffle is almost ideal for "stocking" and "culling," and the curious or interested reader may learn how a perfect knowledge is maintained of the whereabouts of any particular cards, and how they are collected or separated, or placed in any desired positions, while the deck is being shuffled apparently without heed or design.

Primary Accomplishments. — The first acquirement of the professional player is proficiency at "blind" shuffling and cutting. Perfection in performing the "blind" shuffle, whether the old-fashioned hand shuffle or the "riffle" supplemented by a thorough knowledge of "blind" cutting, makes it impossible for the smartest card handler living to determine whether the procedure is true or "blind." This ability once acquired gives the expert ease and assurance in any kind of company, and enables him to lull into a state of absolute serenity the minds of many players who may be naturally suspicious. Nothing so completely satisfies the average card player as a belief that the deck has been thoroughly shuffled and genuinely cut.

Possibilities of the "Blind." — It is surprising to find among card players, and many of them grown gray at the game, the almost universal belief that none but the unsophisticated can be deceived by "blind" shuffling. These gentlemen have to "be shown," but that is the last thing likely to happen. The player who believes he cannot be deceived is in great danger. The knowledge that no one is safe is his best protection. However, the post-graduate in the art is quite conscious of the fact that he himself cannot tell the true from the "blind" shuffle or cut, when performed by another equally as clever. In fact, sight has absolutely nothing to do with the action, and the expert might perform the work just as well if he were blindfolded. Nevertheless "blind" shuffling and cutting, as explained by this work, are among the simplest and easiest feats the professional player is required to perform; and when the process is understood the necessary skill can be acquired with very little time or effort. Given the average card player who can shuffle or "riffle" in the ordinary manner, with some degree of smoothness, he can be taught a "blind" in five minutes that will nonplus the sharpest of his friends. But there are many players who cannot make an ordinary shuffle or "riffle" without bending, breaking, exposing or in some way ruining half the cards, and such bunglers must learn to handle a deck gracefully before attempting a flight to the higher branches of card manipulation.

Uniformity of Action. — The inviolable rule of the professional is uniformity of action. Any departure from his customary manner of holding, shuffling, cutting or dealing the cards may be noticed, and is consequently avoided. The player who uses the old-fashioned hand shuffle will never resort to the table "riffle" in the same company; and vice versa. The manner of holding the deck will always be the same, whether the action is to be true or "blind." In dealing, one particular position for the left-hand fingers is ever adhered to, and the action of the right hand in taking off the cards and the time or rapidity of the dealing is made as uniform as possible. In cutting the rule holds good, and the true cut is made with the same movements as the "blind." Whether the procedure is true or "blind" the same apparent action is maintained throughout.

Deportment. — The deportment of the successful card player must be as finished as his skill. A quiet, unostentatious demeanor and gentlemanly reserve are best calculated to answer his purpose. Especially the entire suppression of emotion over gains or losses. Without ability to control his feelings the "advantage player" is without advantage. Boldness and nerve are also absolutely essential. Ability in card handling does not necessarily insure success. Proficiency in target practice is not the sole qualification of the trap shooter. Many experts with the gun who can nonchalantly ring up the bull's eye in a shooting gallery could not hit the side of a barn in a duel. The greater the emergency, or the greater the stakes, the greater the nerve required.

Display of Ability. — Excessive vanity proves the undoing of many experts. The temptation to show off is great. He has become a past master in his profession. He can laugh at luck and defy the law of chance. His fortune is literally at his finger ends, yet he must never admit his skill or grow chesty over his ability. It requires the philosophy of the stoic to possess any great superiority and refrain from boasting to friend or foe. He must be content to rank with the common herd. In short, the professional player must never slop over. One single display of dexterity and his usefulness is past in that particular company, and the reputation is liable to precede him in many another.

Greatest Single Accomplishment. — If requested to determine from what single artifice the greatest advantage is derived we would unhesitatingly decide in favor of bottom dealing. But skill in that respect would be useless without knowledge of the bottom cards, and to retain them necessitates the ability to "blind" shuffle. Again, the bottom cards may be lost by the cut, hence the necessity of "blind" cutting. Proficiency in palming often takes the place of an ally to "blind" cut, but palming in itself is much more difficult to acquire than "blind" cutting, and is practiced only when the player is alone, and after other ruses, which are less risky, have proven unsuccessful. Hence it will be seen that proficiency in one artifice does not finish the education of the professional card player, and almost every ruse in the game is more or less dependent upon another one.

Effect of Suspicion. — To be suspected of skill is a death blow to the professional. His opportunities are dependent upon belief prevailing among the company he is in that the chances are even. Players may be alert and watchful, which is quite natural in all money games, without disconcerting the expert in the least; but where there is knowledge or even mere suspicion among the players of his ability as a manipulator, it will suggest retirement at once rather than playing against the handicap of being especially watched, and a further possibility of getting his congé from the company. But though under certain circumstances a past-master at the card table may be suspected, detection in any particular artifice is almost impossible, and proof of the act is wholly wanting. For those reasons knowing players require nothing more than a bare suspicion of skill to immediately seek a less misty atmosphere.

Acquiring the Art. — To attain the highest degree of excellence at card manipulation much study and practice are necessary; but proficiency in the art quite sufficient for the purpose of entertainment or amusement may be acquired with very little effort if a thorough understanding is first obtained of the best and simplest methods of accomplishing the sleights. The only proper way to practice is to be seated in the usual manner at a card table with a looking glass opposite; and much time and labor are saved by this plan. The correct positions and movements can be accurately secured, and the performer becomes his own critic.

The beginner invariably imagines his hands are too small or too large, but the size has little to do with the possibilities of skill. Soft, moderately moist hands are best adapted for the purpose. When the cuticle is hard and dry, or excessively humid, the difficulties increase. A simple preparation to soften the hands and good general health usually produce the desired conditions. Of course dry fingers may be moistened, or damp ones dried, but either operation is objectionable.

For superior work the cards should be new, thin, flexible and of best quality. Cheap cards are clumsy and not highly finished. Cards that have been handled two or three hours become more or less sticky, and the slightest friction is a detriment to perfect manipulation.

Importance of Details. — The finished card expert considers nothing too trivial that in any way contributes to his success, whether in avoiding or allaying suspicion, or in the particular manner of carrying out each detail; or in leading up to, or executing, each artifice. Therefore the writer has expended much time and care in illustrating many manœuvres that at first may seem unimportant, but all of which are essential to the curriculum of artistic card handling.

TECHNICAL TERMS

Many of the methods of card manipulation explained in this work originated with us, and we have, in describing the various processes and conditions, used certain terms for the sake of brevity, to designate the particular matters referred to. The reader desiring to follow the action intelligently must clearly understand the meaning of the terms. A careful perusal of the following definitions will save much time and perplexity in comprehending the processes described:

Stock. — That portion of the deck that contains certain cards, placed in some particular order for dealing; or certain desirable cards placed at top or bottom of the deck.

Run. — To draw off one card at a time during the process of the hand shuffle. There is little or no difficulty in acquiring perfect ability to run the whole deck through in this manner with the utmost rapidity. The left thumb presses lightly on the top card, the right hand alone making the movement necessary to shuffle.

Jog. — A card protruding a little from any part of the deck, about a quarter of an inch, to fix the location of any particular card or cards. While shuffling, if the top card is to be jogged, it is pushed over the little finger end of deck by the left thumb, the little finger preventing more than one card from moving. If the first card is to be jogged, that is, the first card in the right hand, it is done by shifting the right hand slightly toward either end of the left-hand packet during the shuffle, so that the first card drawn off by the left thumb will protrude a little over the end of the left-hand packet.

In-Jog. — The card protruding over the little finger of the left hand.

Out-Jog. — The card protruding over the first finger of the left hand.

Break. — A space or division held in the deck. While shuffling it is held at the end by the right thumb. It is formed under the in-jog when about to under-cut for the shuffle, by pushing the in-jog card slightly upward with the right thumb, making a space of from an eighth to a quarter of an inch wide, and holding the space, by squeezing the ends of the packet to be drawn out, between the thumb and second and third fingers. The use of the break during a shuffle makes it possible to throw any number of cards that are immediately above it, in one packet into the left hand, without disarranging their order. The break is used when not shuffling, to locate any particular card or position, and is infinitely superior to the common method of inserting the little finger. A break can be held firmly by a finger or thumb of either hand, and entirely concealed by the other fingers of the same hand. It is also the principal aid in the blind riffles and cuts.

Throw. — To pass from the right hand to the left, during a shuffle, a certain number of cards in one packet, thereby retaining their order. A throw may be required at the beginning, during the process, or at the end of a shuffle; and the packet to be thrown may be located by the jog, or break, or by both.

Culls. — The desired cards. To cull is the act of selecting one or more desired cards, and may consist simply in making the selection as discreetly as possible while gathering up the cards for the deal, or it may be the operation of a much more obscure and apparently impossible feat — that of gathering the desired cards rapidly and easily, from various positions in the deck, to the bottom, during the process of a shuffle that appears perfectly natural and regular.

Blind. — Any method of shuffling, riffling, cutting or culling, designed to appear regular, but in reality retaining, or arranging, some preconceived order.

Upper-Cut. — To take or draw off a packet from the top of the deck.

Under-Cut. — To draw out a packet from the bottom of the deck, during the process of a shuffle.

Run-Cut. — To draw off several or many small packets from the top of the deck.

Top Card. — The card on top of the packet held in the left hand, or the original top card of the full deck, which is about to be shuffled.

First Card. — The card on top of packet held by the right hand to be shuffled.

Shuffle. — The old-fashioned method of shuffling the cards from hand to hand.

Shuffle Off. — To shuffle without design, in the ordinary manner.

Riffle. — The modern method of shuffling on the table by springing the ends of two packets into each other.

Shift. — To return the two portions of the deck to the positions occupied before the cut was made.

Crimp. — To bend one or a number of cards, so that they may be distinguished or located.

ERDNASE SYSTEM OF BLIND SHUFFLES

POSITION FOR SHUFFLE

The deck is held much as usual in the left palm, but more diagonally, so that the first finger from the second joint lies up against the outer end, the first joint of the little finger curled in against the inner end, the second and third fingers slightly curled in against the bottom, and the thumb resting on the top, near the outer end, about the middle. The right hand, when about to shuffle, seizes the under portion at the ends between the thumb and second and third fingers, and the first finger rests on the upper side. (See Fig. 1.) This position, and especially that of the first and little fingers of the left hand, is essential for the process of blind shuffling and stocking. The first and little fingers hold and locate the Jogs, which, in connection with the Break, the Run, and the Throw, make this new mode of stocking and culling possible. The position is easy and quite natural in appearance. There is no strain on the fingers. The deck fits fairly on its side, across the palm, and the left-hand fingers are in much the same position as they would naturally take when the hand is about half closed. It is an excellent manner of holding the deck for the true shuffle, and should be strictly adhered to on all occasions.

BLIND SHUFFLES

The objects of blind shuffling are to retain a top stock, i. e., to retain in the same order the upper portion of the deck which has been prear-ranged for dealing or to retain a bottom stock, which usually consists of

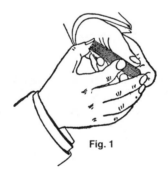

Fig. 1

certain desired cards placed together at the bottom, to be taken from that position at will, during the deal, by bottom dealing; or to retain the whole deck in a certain order, which is rarely attempted, though quite possible. Under the respective headings of "Stocking," and "Culling," it will be learned how the blind shuffle runs up the cards in any desired order, and gathers certain cards from any position to the bottom; but the several methods of retaining the top and bottom stocks are treated separately.

I. To Retain Top Stock

Under-cut about half deck, in-jog first card and shuffle off. Under-cut to in-jog and throw on top.

This is the very simplest form of the blind shuffle and leaves the upper portion of the deck in the same order. The shuffle may be continued ad libitum.

The reader who has prepared himself with a knowledge of the position given for hand shuffling, and the definitions of the list of terms, will have no difficulty in understanding the above directions, and executing the blind at the very first attempt. However, as a first lesson in the A, B, C of card manipulation, the following description of the action is given at length, viz.:

Hold the deck in the manner described for the Shuffle. Seize about half the deck from beneath with the right hand (under-cut), draw out and shift the right hand a little inwards over packet in left hand, so that when the first card is drawn off by the left thumb it will protrude slightly over the little finger (in-jog). Then shuffle off the balance of the cards in the right hand on top of those in the left. (See Fig. 2.) Then seize with

Fig. 2

the right hand all the cards beneath the in-jog card, which protrudes over the little finger of the left hand, and throw them in one packet on top. When seizing the under cards beneath the in-jog, its location is found by the right thumb solely by the sense of touch, and without the least hesitation or difficulty. The in-jog card is held in position by the little finger, and is concealed by the cards on top of it.

The weak point about the foregoing blind is that the last movement is a throw, or under-cut, and it may be noticed that only part of the deck is actually shuffled. This objection is entirely overcome by the use of the break, which is illustrated in the following blind shuffle.

II. To Retain Top Stock and Shuffle Whole Deck

Under-cut about three-quarters of deck, in-jog first card and shuffle off. Under-cut again about three-quarters of deck, forming break at in-jog (see Fig. 3), shuffle off to break and throw balance on top. This blind

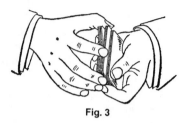

Fig. 3

apparently shuffles the entire deck, but really leaves the top portion in the original order.

There should be no difficulty in forming the break. The right thumb presses slightly upward on the in-jog card when seizing the under portion, and the space created is held by squeezing the ends. It should be done altogether by touch, although from the position it is in, the operator might glance at it without being noticed. It is practically impossible for a spectator to see it unless immediately behind the performer. When shuffling off to the break, the right hand holds the cards firmly and the right thumb gives the warning by the sense of touch when the break is reached. If desired, the right hand may shuffle off, quite carelessly, several cards at a time, and throw the last lot up to the break, by slightly decreasing the pressure on the ends. Above all, a uniformity of time and action must be maintained, though it is not at all essential to the blind to shuffle rapidly.

III. To Retain Bottom Stock and Shuffle Whole Deck

Under-cut about three-quarters of the deck and shuffle off about two-thirds, then in-jog one card and throw balance on top. Under-cut to and include in-jog card (see Fig. 4), and shuffle off.

Fig. 4

This blind retains the bottom stock and apparently shuffles the whole deck. The only difficulty in the action is in including the jog card in the second under-cut. The jog card is pulled back by the thumb, creating a space above it; then as the under-cut is made, the thumb tip is pressed into the opening by squeezing the ends of the under packet, and the upper packet is not disturbed, because the thumbnail slips easily across the card above it as the lower packet is drawn out.

When a jog is formed during the process of any shuffle, and the right hand is shifted a little in or out as the case may be, to allow the jog card to fall in the proper place, the right hand does not at once return to its former position, but gradually works back as the shuffle progresses. This leaves the cards in the left hand a little irregular at the ends, and effectually conceals the fact that any one card is purposely protruding. The ablest shuffler cannot keep his cards quite even, and the irregularity appears even more natural than if in perfect order.

As blind shuffles for retaining the whole deck in its original order are never practiced at the card table, and are only adapted to conjuring purposes, the methods will be found fully explained in the second part of this work.

The foregoing shuffles are simple and easy, and when perfectly performed, absolutely indistinguishable from the true.

ERDNASE SYSTEM OF
BLIND RIFFLES AND CUTS

The riffle, i. e., shuffling the cards on the table by springing the ends of two packets into each other, is by far the more prevalent method in use among regular card players. The possibilities of the riffle, for all practical purposes at the card table, are limited to retaining the top or bottom stock; but in these respects it is quite equal to the hand shuffle as a blind, and the apparent process of thoroughly mixing the cards may be indulged in to any extent without disturbing the order of the top or bottom portion, as the case may be. The order may be arranged to a very limited extent, but the expert who uses the riffle cares little for stocking. His usual procedure is to place the desired cards at the bottom and retain them there. However, if the opportunity has occurred for arranging a top stock, it can be retained during the riffle just as easily. A blind cut should always be alternated with each, or every second riffle.

BLIND RIFFLES

I. To Retain Top Stock

Upper-cut about half the deck with right hand, place two packets end to end on the table in the usual position for riffling. Seize both packets at sides close to adjoining ends between the third finger and thumb of each hand, and rest the hands on the outer ends of packets. Raise the thumb corners, and at the same moment in-jog the top card of the left-hand packet by drawing it in a little over the left thumb, with the first finger of the left hand. The first and second fingers of the left hand conceal both the jog and the action. (See Fig. 5.) Then begin to release, and spring or

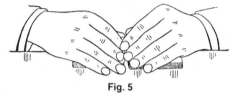

Fig. 5

riffle into each other the ends of the lower cards with both thumbs, but more rapidly with the left thumb, so that the left packet, with the exception of the top card (which is retained on top of the left thumb) will have been riffled in before the right thumb has released the cards of the top stock. Continue the action with the right thumb until all are released, then release last card held by the left thumb. (See Fig. 6.)

This action places one extra card on original top stock. To square up in the ordinary manner would expose the fact that the upper portion had not been riffled. Drop the left thumb on the top card to hold the deck in position and shift the left hand so that the edge of the palm will rest on the table at the end of the left packet and the second and third fingers come along the side. Then with the right hand in much the same

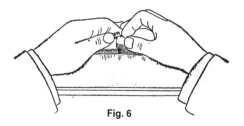

Fig. 6

position as the left, but held more openly, push the right packet in and square up. (See Fig. 7.) Each time this riffle is made it leaves an extra card on top, and the top stock is usually arranged to require two or three extra cards. But if not required the extra card is gotten rid of by blind

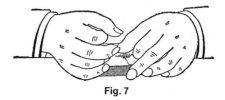

Fig. 7

cut "No. I." After each or every second riffle execute blind cut "No. III To Retain Top Stock."

This riffle, though requiring considerable explanation, is quite simple, and as easily executed as the true. There is no hesitation in the thumb action, although one moves more rapidly than the other. The movements are natural; the positions of the hands are regular, and even the manner of pushing in the cards is the customary one of many players.

But, as intimated, to retain the top stock in the riffle is the exception. In most instances, when the blind is used, it is to retain the bottom stock, and that process which is next described, is even simpler and easier of execution, and more perfect in deception.

II. To Retain Bottom Stock

Upper-cut about half deck with right hand and place the two packets end to end in position for riffle. Seize both packets at sides close to adjoining ends between second finger and thumb of each hand, the third and little fingers curled in, with the first joints resting on top of packets. Raise thumb corners and release bottom stock first with left thumb, then continue action with both thumbs until all cards are riffled in. (See Fig. 8.) Push both packets together in the ordinary manner and square up.

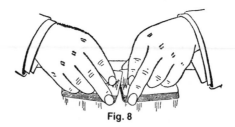

Fig. 8

There is no necessity of covering the bottom stock as in the instance of the top stock, when squaring up; because unless it is very large it is not noticeable, and more than a half dozen cards are rarely held there. However, the same plan used to conceal the top stock may be adopted if desired.

Perhaps a simpler way to perform the blind is to leave the bottom stock on the table without riffling it at all, and the left thumb to pick up the cards above it. The right thumb, of course, picks up the entire right packet. This method prevents any possible difference in the sound of the riffle, though when cleverly performed it is imperceptible to the ear.

This riffle can be varied by drawing out the bottom half with the right hand and leaving, or first releasing, the bottom stock with the right thumb. However, all blind riffling should be occasionally alternated with blind cuts, and when the action is gracefully executed without either haste or hesitation, it is absolutely impossible for any eye to follow the action or detect the ruse. Execute blind cut "No. IV To Retain Bottom Stock" with this riffle.

In performing the Top Stock Riffle, the use of the third fingers and the positions of the hands and other fingers, are very important, as concealment is an essential of the blind. But in the Bottom Stock instance, and especially when the stock is small, the action of not interlacing the bottom cards is not perceptible, and the handling of the deck should be as open and artistic as possible. Hence the use of the second fingers and the curled up positions of the third and little fingers.

Just here we are reminded that comparatively few card players can make an ordinary riffle with any degree of grace or smoothness, and especially few understand how to square up properly. But the whole process is of the simplest nature, and so much easier than clumsy force, if the right method is adopted.

The position given for the Bottom Stock Riffle is the proper one for all ordinary occasions. (See Fig. 8.) The entire work should be done by the second fingers and thumbs. The least possible pressure should be

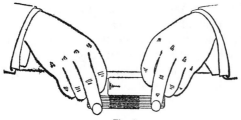

Fig. 9

exerted when springing the corners together, the cards being hardly perceptibly bent. When the corners are interlaced, shift the hands to the outer ends, seizing the side corners with thumbs and second fingers, and telescope the two packets about two-thirds. (See Fig. 9.) Now shift the

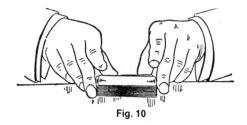

Fig. 10

hands again, bringing the thumbs together at inner side, and a second finger at middle of each end, and square up the deck perfectly by sliding the thumbs outward along the side, and the second fingers inward along the ends (see Fig. 10) until they meet at the corners, squeezing or pressing the cards into position in the action.

The blind process of riffling the two packets truly together, and squaring up in a slightly diagonal position, then withdrawing the packets, throwing the original top one on top again; or pushing the two packets completely through in the diagonal position, leaving the order of the whole deck the same, is quite possible, but very difficult to perform perfectly. But there is seldom a desire and never a necessity of preserving the complete order at a card table, and the foregoing methods are much easier to execute, more perfect as a blind, and answer every purpose.

BLIND CUTS

The blind cut is a natural sequence to the blind shuffle or riffle. As the cards are cut in almost all games, there would be little advantage derived from clever shuffling, were the order to be subsequently disturbed in cutting. The able card handler with a player on his right to blind cut, has the game well in hand. Yet though the advantages are greatly increased by the assistance of an ally, the reader will learn how it is quite possible to play alone and still have a very tolerable percentage of the chances in one's favor. Both hands are invariably used to make a blind cut. The first described is an excellent one for retaining either the top or bottom stock and is in common use among professional players.

I. To Retain Bottom Stock. Top Losing One Card

Seize the deck with left hand at sides, near end, between second finger and thumb, the first finger tip pressing on top. Seize the upper portion of deck with the right hand, at sides, near end, between the second finger and thumb. Raise the deck slightly with both hands and pull out the upper portion with the right hand, but retain the top card in the left hand by pressing on it with the left first finger tip. (See Fig. 11.) Immediately drop the left-hand packet on the table and bring the right-hand packet down on top with a slight swing, and square up.

The action is very simple and easy to execute, the movements are perfectly natural and regular, and, if performed gracefully, is very deceiving. The process displaces the top card, sending it to the middle, and if this blind is used when the top stock is to be retained, an extra card is placed there during the shuffle.

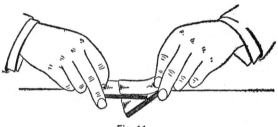

Fig. 11

II. To Retain Complete Stock

The following is a very bold and bare-faced blind, but if cleverly executed it appears natural:

Seize the deck at sides near the ends between the second finger and thumb of each hand, but the left hand seizing the under portion, and the right hand the top portion. Draw out the under portion rapidly with the left hand and place it quickly over towards the dealer, the right hand following slowly and with an upward swing, drops the top portion again on top.

The movements are natural and the blind can be accomplished very neatly. If the plan of drawing off the top portion with the left hand is tried, and then the right following more slowly with the under packet, it will be seen that the identical movements are made in the true cut. It is the movement toward the dealer that makes the blind possible.

III. To Retain Top Stock

The next two methods of blind cuts are among the most subtle and indetectible manœuvers in card handling. The design and use of the break originated with us, and by its aid blind run cuts can be alternated with the blind riffle, until the most critical skeptic will admit that any

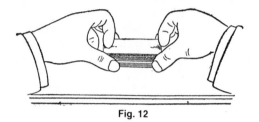

Fig. 12

prearrangement or knowledge of the cards must be hopelessly lost in bewildering confusion.

Seize the deck with both hands, at sides, near the ends, between the thumbs and second fingers; raise it a little from the table and draw off the top stock with the thumb and second finger of the left hand, dropping the left-hand packet on the table, and bring the right-hand packet down on top of it, but retain firm hold with the right hand, and form the break with the right thumb while squaring up the deck. (See Fig. 12.) The left thumb helps to form the break, by holding the space between the two packets while the right thumb is getting the new hold on the whole deck. Then raise the whole deck again with the right hand, and with the left, draw off the upper portion in small packets between the thumb and second finger until the break is reached, dropping the small packets on the table, one on the other (see Fig. 13); and then throw the balance on top with the right hand. This leaves the top stock intact.

Properly performed, it is impossible to detect the ruse. The break is formed on the inside, and at one end only, and is effectually concealed at the end by the right-hand fingers. To see the break the observer would have to be stationed directly behind the operator. The performer him-

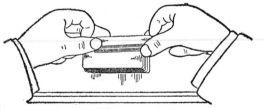

Fig. 13

self cannot see the break, unless his hands are well advanced on the table. When drawing off the small packets, the break is found by the left thumb solely by the sense of touch. The action should not be hurried, and this method of cutting is quite commonly used by many players for the very opposite purpose.

IV. To Retain Bottom Stock

Seize deck at sides, near the ends between the thumb and second finger of each hand, raise a little from the table and draw out the bottom stock with the thumb and finger of the right hand and let the left-hand packet fall on the table. Bring the right-hand packet down on top, retaining the hold until the break is formed by the left thumb, which is held at the edge of the under packet in readiness. Square up the deck and raise it again from the table with both hands; draw off top packet to the break with the left hand and drop it on the table. Then continue the left-hand action, drawing off small packets, dropping them one on the other, and throw the last packet on top with the right hand. This leaves the bottom stock intact. The action is much the same as the preceding blind, the difference being in the position of the break.

It is very important to adopt the proper positions for the fingers in these cuts. The deck should be as much exposed as possible, and the open manner of the whole process makes the blind so much more effective. The cards are handled solely by the second fingers and thumbs. The third fingers are curled up against the ends of the deck and assist in squaring up, and keeping the cards even. The first fingers are curled up on top so as to be out of the way and not obstruct the view.

To form the break, keep the left hand in the position it occupies as it drops the packet on the table, the finger and thumb held open apparently to seize the deck again when the right-hand packet is placed on top. This enables the left thumb to aid in forming the break the instant the two packets are brought together. The right-hand packet is placed on top with a sidling movement instead of straight down, which greatly facilitates the forming of the break, and also prevents the sound from indicating that a space is held. There is nothing difficult about the performance of these blinds. With a perfect understanding, they can be fairly well executed on the first attempt.

This method of blind cutting is particularly adapted for working in with the blind riffle. It appears to assist in mixing the cards, and inspires the most positive conviction of good faith in the performance. The following combination of the riffle and cut will illustrate the point:

COMBINATION RIFFLE AND CUTS

V. To Retain Bottom Stock. Riffle II and Cut IV

Execute Riffle II. Then execute Cut IV. Then Riffle II again. Then draw off with left hand about half the deck in small packets, bring the right hand over on top with the balance, and form a break in squaring up. Then pull out under packet with the right hand and execute Riffle II again. Then pull out a small packet from the middle of deck with the right hand and throw on top. Then draw out about half from the bottom with right hand and form break. Square up, draw out under part again with right hand and execute Riffle II and so on to any extent.

FANCY BLIND CUTS

The next blind described is in common use among advantage players, and while it has an excellent appearance to the uninitiated, we consider it far inferior to Cuts III and IV as a card table ruse. The principal objection is that, once known as a blind, it can never be worked again, as the action is showy and easily recognized.

I. To Retain Complete Stock

Seize the deck at sides, near ends, between second finger and thumb of each hand. Draw out about one-third of deck from bottom with right second finger and thumb, and place on top but retain hold. Then hook up about half of the under part, with the third finger and thumb of right hand, and raise the whole deck from the table with both hands. Now suddenly draw out the middle packet with the right second finger and thumb, and release the top packet with the right second finger, which will allow it to fall on the table. (See Fig. 14.) Drop the left-hand packet on top, and then the right packet.

The hands must be separated rapidly, and with some degree of skill, to allow the top packet to fall fairly on the table, but this is the only hurried

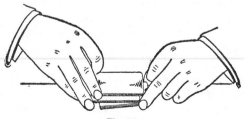

Fig. 14

movement in the cut. The other two packets are thrown on top carelessly and without haste. A little practice is required to execute the ruse gracefully. It is pretty and well worthy of an effort to acquire. We have elaborated upon this cut, and the following formula for a four throw blind is the outcome:

II. To Retain Complete Stock

Seize the deck at sides, near ends, between the second finger and thumb of right hand, and the second and third fingers and thumb of left hand. Draw out about one-quarter of deck from bottom with right hand and place on top, retaining hold. Then slightly raise about one-third of the under packet with the second finger of the left hand, then seize about one-half the remaining lower packet with the third finger of the right hand, holding the last or under portion firmly with the third finger of the left hand. Raise the whole deck from the table and separate both hands suddenly (see Fig. 15), letting the upper packet which is released by the right second finger fall on the table. Then drop lower packet in left hand, then packet in right hand, then last packet in left hand, one on the other, and square up.

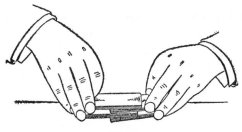

Fig. 15

Some practice is necessary to form the divisions rapidly, and the fingers must take hold of the packets without an instant's delay. The action of dropping the packets one on the other should be rather slow. The appearance of the cut is brilliant, and the fact that the order of the whole deck remains intact will puzzle more than the unsophisticated.

ONE-HANDED FANCY TRUE CUT

A very pretty true cut is made in the following manner. Seize the deck at sides, close to end, so as to expose the whole deck, between the thumb and second and third fingertips of right hand, the fingers close together, but the second fingertip coming only half way down the side. Hook up the top portion with the second fingertip so that the corner will come out free of the third finger, thus dividing the deck in two. (See Fig. 16.) Then give the hand a slight swing or jerk downward and inward, releasing the upper portion with the second finger, allowing it to fall on the table. Then drop under portion on top. In seizing the deck, if it is slid to the table edge and tilted over slightly, the thumb and fingers take hold much easier, and are certain of raising all the cards. In making this cut the deck is held but a few inches from the table, and the action must be nicely made to have the cards fall flatly. The run cut can be made in

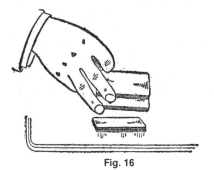

Fig. 16

the same way, dropping the packets one on the other. The action is the same when the cut is made by seizing the ends, but it is a little more difficult. No haste should be taken. The movements should be deliberate, so that the truth of the cut is apparent. The only advantage the cut possesses is its beauty, and a possible aid at times, by giving an excuse to square up with both hands. The run cut is liable to leave the cards uneven, and a left palm hold out can be replaced in this way. The only drawback is the danger in making a display of even such simple ability.

TO INDICATE THE LOCATION FOR THE CUT

While on the subject of cuts, we shall consider the various methods by which a true cut can be made by an ally, and still leave the complete stock intact. The dealer prepares for this by making an extra cut when his shuffle is completed, and indicates by one of the following methods the point at which he wishes his ally to reverse his last action, by making a true cut.

I. *This is located by the crimp.* — When using the hand shuffle make an extra under-cut of about half the deck, and when throwing the under packet on top shift the right hand slightly inward and form an in-jog,

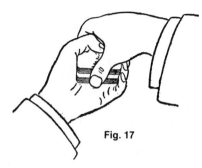

Fig. 17

the left little finger helping to hold the location between the two packets. Then turn the left hand slightly downward, bringing the right hand over on top of the deck, and seize the ends between thumb and second and third fingers, apparently to square up. As the right thumb comes against the inner end it pulls up the in-jog slightly, forming a break. (See Fig. 17.) Then with the fingers of left hand crimp, or squeeze the under packet against palm of hand so as to leave the under packet slightly concave. (See Fig. 18.) The right hand effectively conceals this action of the left. Lay the deck down perfectly square to be cut. The ally makes the cut at the ends with one hand, and locates the crimp by touch. There is little or no difficulty in finding the crimp. It is the most

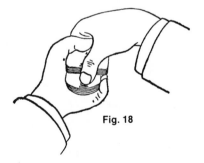

Fig. 18

probable place the cut would be made, even if left to chance, and many an unsophisticated player has unconsciously cut into a crimp and aided in his own undoing. If the deck is placed before an innocent player so that his hand naturally seizes the ends, the chances are in favor of his cutting to the opening. (See Fig. 19.) A professional will calculate on this probability when his right-hand neighbor is not an ally. The main

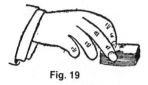

Fig. 19

objection to the crimp is that the bent cards may be noticed. The dealer immediately crimps in the opposite direction when squaring up after the cut.

The same result can be achieved by putting in a convex crimp in the under portion. It is led up to in the same manner, and the first finger of the left hand aids in forming the crimp by being curled up and pressed against the under packet to bend it upwards. In this case the ally cuts at the sides, and locates the crimp accurately by pressing the second or third fingertip on the top near the outside edge. This tilts the upper packet a little, and enables the thumb to find the crimp without an instant's hesitation. (See Fig. 20.)

Fig. 20

II. *This is located by the jog.* — When using the hand shuffle change the position slightly so that the four fingers will lie flatly against the bottom of the deck. Make the extra under-cut and bring tips of the second and third left fingers in against and slightly above packet remaining in left hand. In throwing the right-hand packet on top, let it slide a little across the left fingertips, so that a jog is made by the bottom card or cards, which are prevented from going completely over. (See Fig. 21.) This is perfectly hidden by the right hand. Square up the deck by the ends only and lay down to be cut, thereby not disturbing the jog. The ally cuts with the left hand, seizing the upper packet by the sides, the left thumb easily and instantaneously locating the jog by touch.

The action of both players must be rapid and careless in appearance, but not hurried. The irregularity of the side edges made necessary by the jog does not attract attention or expose the ruse, as in ordinary play the deck is rarely perfectly square when given to cut.

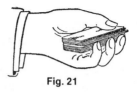

Fig. 21

III. This is located by the crimp. — When the riffle is used, the crimp is put in by first concaving the whole deck. This is a natural procedure, as the cards have a tendency to get convex, and it is quite customary for the players to straighten them up. By drawing the deck to the edge of the table the concave tendency can be put in the whole deck first, then as the extra cut is made a convex crimp can be put in the under part by pressing it quickly downward with right thumb against the table edge as it is drawn out. The ally cuts by the ends.

IV. This is located by the jog. — Perhaps the best manner of locating the cut when the riffle is used, is to jog the top card by pushing it slightly over the right-hand end, with the left first finger. Then make the extra cut with the right hand, throwing the under portion on top, and squaring up at sides and left-hand end only. The deck is passed to the ally by the sides with the right hand, which conceals the jogged card. The ally cuts by the ends, his thumb easily locating the jog, and seizing the packet above it.

The particular manner in which the dealer forms the crimp, or jog, to locate the cut, matters little if it is done in a natural manner and without attracting attention. But a single irregular movement, or a moment's hesitation, may ruin the play. Hence, however simple and easy the particular action may be, the execution should be carefully planned and practiced beforehand, and when put into effect should be performed almost mechanically. For these reasons we have devoted much space to many details that may at first appear of little moment.

BOTTOM DEALING

The art of dealing from the bottom, although not the most difficult to attain, is perhaps the most highly prized accomplishment in the repertory of the professional. The bottom is the most convenient place for retaining desirable cards during the shuffle or riffle, and perfection in dealing from that position obviates to a great extent the necessity of stocking, as the cards can be dealt at will, and consequently need not be run up in a certain order. Like acquiring many other feats, a perfect understanding of the exact manner in which it is performed will avoid the principal difficulties. Practice will soon do the rest.

Hold the deck in the left hand, resting one corner against the middle of the first joint of the second finger, the other corner of the same end in the second joint of the first finger, the first two joints of which rest idly along end of deck. Press the deck outward as much as possible and rest the opposite inner end corner against the palm below the base of thumb. Rest the thumb on the top of deck, pointing toward the second finger-tip, which just shows at top of corner. Bring up little finger against the side, and the third finger midway between the second and little fingers. The deck is held in position principally by the corners, between the second finger and the palm below base of thumb. The little finger may aid in holding the deck, but it must be released when the bottom card is pushed out. (See Fig. 22.)

Fig. 22

The second finger and thumb do the work. Draw back the thumb a little and push the top card over in the usual position to seize with the right hand for dealing. Then draw back the third finger, which action is concealed by the overhanging card, until the tip rests against the edge of the bottom card. (See Fig. 23.) Press up and slightly inward against that

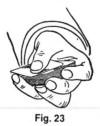

Fig. 23

card and push it out, at same time releasing the little finger and holding the deck firmly between second finger and palm. If this is done properly it leaves the top and bottom cards in the same relative position, the top card effectively concealing the under one. Now advance the right hand apparently to take off the top card. (See Fig. 24.) Draw back the top card with the left thumb, and at the same instant seize the bottom card instead with the right thumb and second finger and deal it in the usual manner. (See Fig. 25.) This can be done so perfectly that the quickest eye cannot detect the ruse. It requires some practice. The main thing is to understand the action thoroughly and hold the deck correctly.

The position is an excellent one for ordinary dealing, and should never be changed. The corner pressed against the palm should be as far from the wrist as possible. Each time a card is pressed out from the

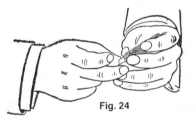

Fig. 24

bottom, the deck will have a tendency to slip toward the wrist, and must be held, or worked back into position again.

The left hand does nine-tenths of the work. After the hold is established, the main task is in acquiring facility to push out the bottom card with the second fingertip. The cards may come out in numbers, or appear to stick fast; but the process is very easy when the knack is once obtained. The second fingertip comes around the corner to the side, just barely sufficiently to hold the deck in place, and when the third fingertip releases the bottom card from the hold of the second finger, it slips out quite freely. The thumb of the left hand plays a very important part in the blind, by drawing back the top card at the proper instant; and it is this action that makes the deal appear perfectly regular. The thumb movement is identically the same as in the true deal, and the drawing back of the top card is undetectable when properly and rapidly executed. A very slight up and down movement of the left hand as the cards are taken, aids in concealing the action. Hoyle makes a point of instructing that a dealer should always keep the outer end of the deck, and the cards, as dealt, inclined toward the table. Following this rule tends to hide the work of the third finger in bottom dealing.

Bottom dealing is little used with a full deck. It becomes much easier as the pack grows less, consequently the dealer waits until the last several rounds before resorting to it. It is also easier to deal the cards alternately

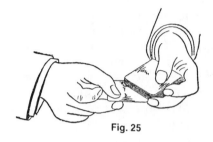

Fig. 25

from the top and bottom than to take them from the bottom one after the other. The movement of the third finger need not be so rapid and is less noticeable; and should the deck slip out of position, it can be worked back as the top card is being taken. When the bottom cards must be taken consecutively, it is an aid to crimp them very slightly, or to jog them a little, i. e., to allow them to protrude about an eighth of an inch at the side. But neither of the manœuvers is desirable, or necessary to a good performer.

TOP AND BOTTOM DEALING WITH ONE HAND

This is a very pretty method of varying the deal, and carries certain advantages with it. The deck is held in exactly the same manner as described for bottom dealing. The single-handed top deal is made by pushing over the top card with the thumb in the usual manner, and then with a swing of the hand toward the player, the card is released by the thumb and slides off the deck over the table in the direction indicated. The single-handed bottom deal is made by first pushing over the top card as usual, then instead of pushing out the bottom card, as in the two-handed deal, it is sprung back a little by the third fingertip, and then suddenly sprung forward and out as the hand is swung in the direction of the player.

This bottom deal is really more deceptive than where the two hands are employed, as it appears so open, and the action is completely hidden by the natural swing of the hand necessarily made towards the player, to cause the card to slide in the proper direction. The action of the wrist is a little varied as the cards are dealt to the left, opposite or to the right; and the impetus and direction given to each card must be nicely calculated to make the deal appear graceful. Unless the cards fall pretty fairly before each player, it would seem very awkward indeed. The swing, and the wrist action, for dealing the top and bottom cards, are just about the same.

Single- and double-handed top and bottom card dealing can be nicely combined, and has an advantage over the exclusive use of the one or the other. If the bottom cards are intended for, say, the third player from the dealer, he can deal the first two top cards single-handed, and then bring up the right hand and continue the rest of the round double-handed, giving the third player the bottom card as the hands are first brought together. Each round should be made in the same uniform manner. The advantage in this procedure is, that when the bottom card is wanted the dealer's hands are separated possibly eight or ten inches, and the movement required to bring them together covers up and gives time for the action of the left hand in getting the top and bottom cards in position. The finished expert can deal the bottom cards at will, under any circumstances, without a possibility of detection; but it is our desire to show the most favorable conditions under which the ruse can be employed. The single- and double-handed deal is quite frequently used by players who know absolutely nothing about advantages. It looks pretty, the movements are natural, and the change of pace causes no suspicion.

When dealing Stud Poker, or turning a trump, the average player takes off the cards that are to be faced, by inverting the right hand, and seizing them with the fingers on top and thumb under, thereby turning the cards before they completely leave the left hand. This must not be attempted if the bottom card is to be dealt or turned trump. The inverted position of the hand makes it more difficult to get the bottom card out noiselessly. The cards should be taken in the usual manner by the right hand, and turned the instant they are quite free of the deck.

SECOND DEALING

As the term indicates, second dealing is the process of dealing the second card from the top, and it is employed almost exclusively in connection with marked cards. It is obvious that the dealer will possess a very great advantage by being enabled to reserve for himself, or an ally, any desirable cards as they appear at the top. He need not bother about acquiring skill at blind shuffling, cutting stocking, or any of the other hundred and one ruses known to the profession.

The deck is held by the left hand much the same as described for bottom dealing, the tip of the thumb being a little over the end of the top card. This position enables the thumb to come in contact with the second card by pushing the top card a trifle downwards. To deal, the left thumb pushes the two cards over the side nearly together, the top card perhaps a little in advance and the second card showing a little above it at the end. The right hand seizes the second card by the exposed corner, the right thumb barely touching the edge, but the right second finger is well under the second card and helps to get it out by an upward pressure as the left thumb draws back the top card. (See Fig. 26.) Then the left thumb again comes in contact with the second card at the upper edge. The third fingertip prevents more than two cards from being pushed over the side. The top card continues to move forward and back as the seconds are dealt, but the rapidity of the backward movement prevents the detection of the action. Properly executed, the appearance of the deal is perfectly regular. An expert can run the whole deck with the utmost rapidity, and still retain the top card.

Another method of second dealing is to hold the cards loosely in the left hand, the left thumb pushing forward several at a time, each a little in advance of the other. As the right hand comes forward, the top card is

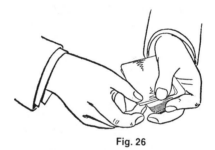

Fig. 26

drawn back and the second dealt. The left thumb uses some pressure in pushing the cards forward, but draws back the top card very lightly so as to have the second card protruding. (See Fig. 27.) The first method is

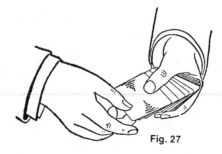

Fig. 27

decidedly the better, as it gives greater control of the cards, and there is less liability of the right hand seizing more than one. There is a knack in seizing the second card. The second finger of the right hand comes in contact with it before the top card is drawn back, and gives it a slight pressure upward, thus helping to prevent it going back with the top card. The right thumb may actually touch the top card as it is drawn back and the second dealt. The whole action of drawing back the top and dealing the second card takes place at the same instant.

To become an adept at second dealing is as difficult a task as can be given in card handling, but once acquired, like many other arts, it is as easy as habit. To the player who uses marked cards this accomplishment is the whole thing, but without "readers" the time spent in acquiring the skill is wasted as far as advantage playing is concerned. Opportunities for introducing prepared cards are rare, and the process of marking during a game, by crease, crimp, or inking, is slow and detectable. However, with "readers," "strippers," or any kind of prepared cards the clever professional who values his reputation will have nothing to do.

ORDINARY METHODS OF STOCKING, LOCATING AND SECURING

The most ordinary mode of stocking consists in arranging the cards as discreetly as possible while taking tricks, or making the discard, or while gathering up for the deal. There is no sleight of hand in this. A player, if he keeps his wits about him, finds many opportunities during a sitting of prearranging to some extent for his deal. With the aid of a partner of course the possibilities are doubled. But the general understanding is that the whole deck must be tampered with before the shuffle begins. If dalliance with the deck is allowed — and it is amazing how much of that sort of thing is permitted in some games — a practiced operator can run up one or two hands with incredible rapidity, and his actions will appear as mere trifling.

This is done by holding the deck in the left hand, back to palm, with thumb against one side, second, third and little fingers on the other side, and first finger curled up against the back. The right hand now covers the face, fingers at one end, thumb at the other. The left thumb then springs the cards so that the index can be seen. (See Fig. 28.) As a desired card is located, the lower side of the deck is opened at that point, and the left second, third and little fingers inserted, and the

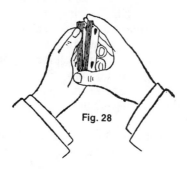

Fig. 28

card is drawn or slipped out to the top of deck. (See Fig. 29.) Then indifferent cards to the requisite number are slipped from the bottom in the same manner on top of the first selected card. Then the next desired card is located and brought to the top, and so on till the stock is complete. Little or no skill is required, but a practiced hand can locate and bring the cards to the top in a moment or two and without the least noise.

Fig. 29

Two sets of threes for a Poker game may be stocked with but four movements, if the desired cards happen to be separated. Assume the game is five-handed. The dealer glances at the index of the five top cards, or places his own hand on top for the start, and finds, say, Six, Four, Queen, Nine and Eight. He decides to run up three Fours for the second player, and three Eights for himself. He springs the cards until he locates an Eight, then inserts second and third fingers, then springs the next two indifferent cards and inserts the little finger, and slips these three cards to the top. Then he locates a Four and the next indifferent card and brings these to the top. Then the Eight again, with two cards; then the Four with one card, and the stock is complete. It would take an untutored player ten times as long to set up the hands if he had the deck, table and room all to himself.

A more artistic method of locating and securing cards, when the company will stand for dalliance at all, is to jog the desired cards and bring them to the bottom with one movement when about to riffle. It can be accomplished in the following manner:

Hold the deck in the left hand, back to palm, between thumb and fingers, as described for the last process, but in covering the face with the right hand bring the first three fingers straight across the outer end of the deck, the little finger against the lower side at corner and the thumb on top side at corner close to right first finger. Then spring the cards with the left thumb against right thumb. When a desired card is located tilt the packet, then held between the right thumb and little finger, about half an inch outward, so that the right thumb will pass the corner of the packet held by the left hand. (See Fig. 30.) Then release the desired card with the left thumb, press down on its corner with the right thumb and bring the right-hand packet back to its original position, closing up the space entirely. In doing so it will force the desired card down and out against the left-hand fingers. Release these fingers slightly as the packets are being closed, and then press the desired card up again with the left

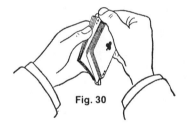

Fig. 30

little finger. This will cause it to protrude about half an inch at the end, but it is entirely concealed by the positions of the hands. The deck can now be again sprung rapidly with the left thumb in search of the next card without disturbing the one already jogged, and the procedure be repeated until the required number are jogged in the position of the first. (See last Figure.) When toying with the deck is tolerated, no more innocent-appearing action can be taken. The movements to jog the cards are imperceptible if cleverly executed, and it is quite apparent to an onlooker that the relative positions of the cards are not changed. The fact that the springing is continued after the cards are jogged, and the visible end and the sides of the deck are squared up perfectly before the riffle begins, make it appear to even a suspicious observer that any knowledge of location would be again lost.

When the desired cards are jogged, jog several of the top cards at the same end, concealing their opposite ends with the right fingers, then shift the left thumb and second and third fingers to the inner side corners, and turn the deck face down, shifting the right hand to the top

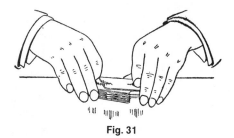

Fig. 31

at the opposite side corners in position to make a running cut. Then with the left hand draw off the top packet, sliding out the jogged cards with the same movement, dropping them on the table (see Fig. 31), and make a running cut with the rest of the deck. This leaves the desired cards at the bottom.

There is no difficulty at all in the action of getting out the jogged cards. A firm hold on them is obtained by the left fingers, and they are concealed by the packet coming off the top. If the action of jogging the cards is not suspected the rest is easy and absolutely undetectable. Three or four cards can be located and brought to the bottom in this manner in ten seconds. The blind riffle is at once proceeded with in the usual way to retain bottom stock.

A complete Top Stock may be run up by the last method if the cards chance to be separated. Assuming again that the game is Five-Handed Poker, and say Three of a Kind are desired. When the first card is located the next four indifferent cards are sprung and the five jogged all together with one movement. Then the next card is located, four added and jogged. But when the third card of the Kind is located but only two indifferent cards are added. Then when about to riffle, the jogged cards are drawn out as in the last described process, but thrown on top instead of on the table. This action appears like a simple cut. Now the "Top Stock Blind Riffle" is executed twice, which action places two additional cards on top, and these are necessary to complete the Top Stock and give the Three of a Kind to the dealer.

As mentioned, the desired Three must chance to be separated by at least the four cards necessary to go in between them. However, the probabilities are that even Four of a Kind will be found so removed. It is very simple to run up Flushes in this manner, and in nine cases out of ten any suit will be found sufficiently dispersed. It is very easy to count the cards rapidly and accurately, if the position for holding the deck is properly maintained; and the action is the same in running up a stock for any game.

STOCK SHUFFLE

Running up the desired cards in a certain order for dealing, while the deck is being shuffled, can be accomplished to any considerable extent only by the hand shuffle. The method in common use by expert players is to draw the particular cards from the bottom. This method is first explained.

Seize the deck at ends between the second finger and thumb of the right hand in the usual manner for shuffling, the first finger resting on the side. Run several cards into the left hand, but well down into the palm, so that the second and third fingers protrude to the first joints from underneath. Then when the right hand has made the next downward motion, instead of drawing off the top card with the left thumb press the left second and third fingertips against the bottom card and let it slide

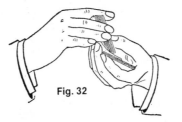

Fig. 32

into the left hand, drawing it into position on the other cards with the left thumb as the right hand is raised. (See Fig. 32.) The right hand aids the left fingers by pressing the deck against them and drawing up more horizontally. Then run one card less than the number of players and again draw one from the bottom, and so on until the stock is complete. The left thumb goes through the same motion when the under card is drawn, but merely slides across the top card without disturbing it. When the last card has been drawn from the bottom run as many cards as there are players between the dealer and the player for whom the bottom cards are intended, out-jog the next card and shuffle off balance. Then under-cut to out-jog and throw on top.

This example, of course, is for a game in which the cards are dealt one at a time to each player. If the game requires two or more cards at a time the action is the same but merely repeated. The right hand makes the movement of shuffling, on the same plane, or about parallel with the packet held in the left, and this aids in drawing the bottom cards, as well as disguising that action. There is a little difference in the sound as the cards fall from the top and bottom, but it is hardly noticeable. This method requires considerable practice, as the knack of drawing the bottom cards, and but one at a time, does not come easily. But when acquired it can be executed with wonderful facility and speed, and the ruse is practically undetectable. The shuffle may be continued to any length by under-cutting below the stock, jogging the first card, shuffling off and then again under-cutting to jog and throwing on top; or the blind top stock, apparent shuffle of the whole deck, may be made as described in this work.

Two or more hands may be run up by this method, if one set is placed at the top and the other at the bottom. The process is to first draw from the top, then from the bottom, in succession, until all the selected cards have been arranged alternately at the bottom of the left-hand packet, then shuffle off balance. Then run several cards from the top for a start, and then draw the first card from the bottom. Then run from the top the number that there are players between where the first bottom card is to fall, and where the second one is intended. Then draw again from the bottom, and so on until the two sets have been run up. The calculation is very simple and of course should be made beforehand. For instance, in a five-handed game of Poker assume that three Queens and three Nines are to be stocked. The Queens are to go to the man who cuts, and the Nines to the second player from the dealer. Place the Queens on top, the Nines under. Run Queen, then draw a Nine, and so on until all are under the deck. Then the calculation would be, on every five cards that are shuffled, to draw the second and fourth from the bottom. The cards must be run up in the reverse order, so the count is made to the right, the dealer being first. His card comes from the top. Then the second card from the bottom, which is the Queen, then the third from the top, then the fourth from the bottom, which is the Nine, then the fifth and first again from the top, then the second from the bottom, and so on until fifteen cards have been run. Then out-jog and shuffle off. Then under-cut to jog and throw on top.

The ability of drawing the bottom cards smoothly and rapidly must be perfectly acquired before this method of stocking can be successfully used. The most that can be said for it is that it is short. A single hand can be run up with one shuffle and a throw. By executing the blind top stock shuffle, after the stock is run up, any awkwardness in the first process may be covered. Success in all card achievements depends on avoiding or allaying suspicion, and the blind shuffles described, if properly performed, will satisfy the most exacting.

ERDNASE SYSTEM OF STOCK SHUFFLING

The common method of stocking which has just been explained is very simple and easy to understand but extremely difficult to execute perfectly. The principal objections are that drawing from the bottom is an unnatural movement, that it requires much skill to accomplish the feat gracefully, and a great deal of practice to acquire the skill, and that this difficult and unnatural movement has to be executed for every card that is put in the stock, thereby increasing the chances of attracting attention when the stock is large. The new method about to be described is infinitely easier of execution, and the movements are so natural and regular that a very indifferent performer can defy the closest scrutiny. The cards may be shuffled with the utmost rapidity, or worked in quite slowly, without fear of exposing the action. The time required is not greater than usually taken in an ordinary shuffle, and the calculations are simple.

The principal aids in this new method are the jogs and the break, and they are used to hold and separate and locate solely by the sense of touch, the various divisions created during the shuffle. The entire stock is run up independent of sight, and, in fact, the dealer can no more follow the action with his eyes than can those who are most interested in scrutinizing his work. We will give as a first illustration the action required for stocking two cards in any game that is dealt one card at a time to each player. The position given for shuffling must be maintained.

Two-Card Stock. — The two desired cards are placed on top, under-cut about half the deck, in-jog top card, run two less than twice the number of players, out-jog and shuffle off. Under-cut to out-jog, forming break at in-jog; run one less than number of players, in-jog and shuffle off. Under-cut to in-jog and throw on top. This action places the two desired cards so that they will fall to the dealer in the first two rounds.

The reader who has mastered the blind shuffles should find it a very simple matter to perform this stock. His knowledge of the terms must be clear, and he must have the slight skill necessary to make the run, jog, break, and throw, as required in the blind shuffles. If a perfect understanding of this simple stock is obtained it will make the whole subject easy of comprehension. We will describe the action at length.

Assuming that it is a five-handed poker game. Two Kings, the desired cards, which are placed on top. The first action is to "under-cut about half the deck," then "in-jog top card;" that is, to push one of the Kings slightly over the little finger end of the left-hand packet with the left

Fig. 33

thumb. It is done the instant the under-cut is made, and just before the right hand makes the downward motion to shuffle. "Run two less than twice the number of players," which would be eight; "out-jog," that is, run the next card out over the left first finger by shifting the right hand slightly outward, "and shuffle off," which means to shuffle the balance of the right-hand packet into the left hand without design. The left little and first fingers now hold the in and out-jogs. (See Fig. 33.)

The next operation is, "Under-cut to out-jog, forming break at in-jog." The right-hand fingers easily find the out-jog, the right thumb presses up a little on the in-jog card, and forms and holds a space, as the under packet is drawn out. (See Fig. 34.) "Run one less than number of players," four, "throw to break," that is, pass the rest of the cards above the break in one packet into the left hand, which is done by lessening the right thumb pressure somewhat and slightly accelerating the down-

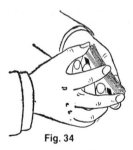

Fig. 34

ward motion. (See Fig. 35.) "Run number of players," five, "in-jog and shuffle off." The in-jog is made in this instance by shifting the right hand inward so that the card drawn off by the left thumb will fall slightly over the little finger. Then "under-cut to in-jog, and throw on top" will be understood.

The only action in any of the formulas for this method of stocking that

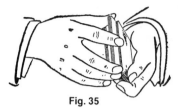

Fig. 35

will be found at all difficult is that of jogging the top card. It must be done rapidly and just at the moment the right hand is descending to shuffle.

Three-Card Stock. — Any game in which cards are dealt singly. Three desired cards on top. Under-cut about half deck, in-jog top card, run two less than twice the number of players, out-jog and shuffle off. Under-cut to out-jog, forming break at in-jog; run one less than number players, throw to break, run one, in-jog running one less than twice number of players, out-jog and shuffle off. Under-cut to in-jog and throw on top. Under-cut to out-jog, run one less than number of players and throw balance on top. This gives the dealer the three desired cards in three rounds.

In the second shuffle of this stock where directed to "in-jog running one less than number players," the in-jog card is counted in the run. "Under-cut to in-jog and throw on top" is to make a simple cut of the deck below the in-jog card.

Four-Card Stock. — For any game in which cards are dealt singly. Three of the desired cards are placed on top, one on bottom. Under-cut about one-third deck, in-jog top card, run two less than twice number players, out-jog and shuffle off to last card, so that it will be left on top. Under-cut to out-jog, forming break at in-jog, run one less than number players, throw to break, run one, in-jog running one less than twice number players, out-jog and shuffle off. Under-cut to in-jog and throw on top. Under-cut to out-jog, run one less than number players and throw balance on top. This gives the four desired cards to the dealer in four rounds.

The action of shuffling the last card on top is not at all difficult. A little practice enables the right hand to release all but the bottom card with ease and accuracy. It must be done quite frequently, and the knack can be acquired without trouble.

In the examples given the selected cards are stocked to fall to the dealer, but of course this is not always desired. It is just as simple to give them to any player by adding to or taking from the top, which may be done by varying the original calculation or by continuing a blind shuffle. If one card is taken from the top the player on the right gets the cards. If one is added they go to the player on the left, and so forth.

The stock must be run up without hurry or hesitation, at the dealer's customary gait. Rapidity is not essential, but smoothness and uniformity are. The break is formed, and the jogs are found, in the usual time necessary for drawing out the under-cut. To go through the whole stock slowly is much better than to change the pace. The four-card stock for five players can be run up in fifteen seconds or less, but there is no reason why much greater time should not be taken.

The philosophy of the action may be reasoned out or not, as the student sees fit; but in any case to accomplish the stock gracefully and expeditiously he must not stop in the middle of the shuffle to calculate. The formula and figures must be literally at his fingers' ends. Most players stick to one or two games, and a little practice at that particular stock makes it as easy as habit. The highest tribute that can be paid to the method is the fact that certain players whom we have instructed, can execute the stock with the greatest facility and yet confess they cannot tell why the particular action produces the result, and they are totally unable to see what becomes of the selected cards until the shuffle is completed. However, it requires no feat of memory, and a few repetitions of the same formula enables one to stock and talk at the same time.

Five-Card Stock. — For any game in which cards are dealt singly. Four desired cards on top, one on bottom. Under-cut about one-third deck, in-jog top card, run two less than twice number players, out-jog and shuffle last card on top. Under-cut to out-jog, forming break at in-jog; run one less than number players, throw to break, run two, in-jog one and shuffle off. Under-cut to in-jog and throw on top. Under-cut about one-third deck, in-jog top card, run two less than twice number players, out-jog and shuffle last card to top. Under-cut to out-jog, forming break at in-jog; run one less than number players, throw to break, run three times number players, in-jog and shuffle off. Under-cut to in-jog and throw on top. This gives the dealer the five cards in five rounds.

The formula appears long, but much of the shuffle is a repetition, very simple, and takes but a second or two longer than the four-card stock.

To show the possibilities of this method, we give a fancy stock for a game of Poker that will throw Four of a Kind to the dealer and leave two sets of fours on the top for the draw.

Twelve-Card Stock. — For Draw Poker. Three sets of fours on top, the set for the dealer to be the under-most. Take whole deck in right hand, run nine and throw balance on top, forming in-jog with throw. Under-cut about one-third deck, forming break at in-jog, in-jog top card, run two less than twice number players, out-jog, shuffle off to break and throw on top. Under-cut to out-jog, forming break at in-jog, run one less than number players, throw to break, run one, in-jog running one less than three times number players, out-jog and shuffle off. Under-cut to in-jog and throw on top. Under-cut to out-jog, run one less than number players and throw on top. This gives the dealer the first of his set of four on the second round, and leaves the other two sets on top for the draw. If the dealer's set is the highest of the three it matters little to him how the draw is made, as none of the players can get a better hand even by drawing four.

The action is the same as the four-card stock, with the exception of the first shuffle, which arranges three of the dealer's set on the top, and his fourth card at the break on top of the other two sets. Then — as in the next shuffle the break is thrown on top — it brings the dealer's set in precisely the same position as the first shuffle in the four-card stock. The balance of the action is the same only that the second under-cut shuffle in-jogs one less than three times number players, instead of one less than twice number players; and this is done to put the extra number of cards in the stock so that the five rounds may be dealt and leave the other sets intact for the draw.

We term this example a fancy stock, as it is very rarely that an opportunity occurs for selecting three sets of Four of a Kind; but the procedure is the same for two sets, or for sets of three, or pairs, or, in fact, for the stocking of any number or kind, with slight variation in the calculation.

The foregoing illustrations of stocking are applicable for Whist, Hearts, Poker, Cribbage and all games wherein the cards are dealt singly. It is much simpler to stock when the cards are dealt two or more at a time, and in this class are Euchre, Coon Can, Penuckle, varieties of All Fours, Piquet, etc. We shall illustrate the simplicity of a Euchre Stock. The hungriest dealer would not desire more than four cards, as in nine cases out of ten it will give him a lone hand.

Euchre Stock. — Four-handed game. Four desired cards on top. Under-cut about three-quarters of deck, run seventeen, in-jog and shuffle off. Under-cut to in-jog and throw on top. This will give three of the desired cards to the dealer and turn the fourth for trump. The dealer takes two cards the first round and three on the last, thereby getting three of the desired cards on the last round and turning the fourth for trump. The calculation is in merely counting the number of cards required in the deal before reaching the desired cards, which are for the dealer and the trump. In a three-handed game the run would be twelve — i. e., five less. In a two-handed game, seven. As described above, the shuffle is too short. A blind shuffle should be first executed, leaving the desired cards on top, and then the stock run up. If the two bowers are among the desired cards the left must not be turned for trumps, so it may be placed at any position among the desired cards save the under one.

If the desired cards are to be given to the dealer's partner the action is almost as short.

Euchre Stock. — Four-handed game. Four desired cards on top for partner and trump. Under-cut about three-quarters of deck, in-jog top card, run sixteen, out-jog and shuffle off. Under-cut to out-jog, forming break at in-jog, in-jog first card running eleven, throw to break, run three and shuffle off. Under-cut to in-jog and shuffle off. This gives the player opposite the dealer three of the desired cards on the second round, and turns the fourth card for trumps.

For the benefit of the reader who wishes to understand the philosophy of the procedure, we will explain the calculation fully. We must first determine how the desired cards must stand when the shuffle is completed. The order for dealing the first round is, three, two, three, two; and the second round two, three, two, three. Now, to give his partner three desired cards on the second round they must stand the thirteenth, fourteenth and fifteenth cards from the top, and the fourth desired card must stand the twenty-first from the top to turn for trumps. It would be easy to stock from these figures, but there is a shorter way. As there are only thirty-two cards in the Euchre deck, the desired cards must be nearer the bottom than the top, so if we count from the bottom we will find the trump card is the twelfth, with five indifferent cards between it and the other three desired cards. The eleven cards below the trump and the five above give us the number sixteen, which is the first run in the shuffle. The second run in the shuffle is eleven, which action makes the division, and the rest of the action is for the purpose of inserting the desired cards in the divisions created.

Any one who can understand and execute the Euchre examples, should have no trouble in stocking for any of the other games wherein two or more cards are dealt at a time. The more at a time the simpler to run up more desired cards. But two good cards on each deal are quite sufficient to turn the tide strongly in favor of the advantage player, and for practical purposes stocking more than three should not be attempted. Simple ability to make the run and the in-jog, enables one to stock two or three cards in any game that deals two or three at a time.

ERDNASE SYSTEM OF CULL SHUFFLING

In most card games where there is a stake at issue the scrutiny is so close and the rules are so strict, that the expert card handler finds little opportunity to make an open selection of any particular cards. The slightest action that indicates such a purpose invites suspicion, and there is an old adage much quoted that runs, "If suspected, quit." However, we shall describe a new method of making many selections without a possibility of the design being detected, and in a manner so natural and regular that not a movement is made that indicates anything more than the purpose of thoroughly shuffling the deck.

The necessary preparation for the cull shuffle is to note at what particular number the first of the desired cards will stand from the top when thrown on the deck, and at what number the next will stand from the first, and so on for as many cards as are to be culled. For instance, if there are three desired cards, the first the eighth from the top, the next the fourth from that, and the next the sixth card further down, their order is fixed in the mind as eight, four, six. The lowest desired card is eighteenth card from the top of the deck, but the count is made from one desired card to the other. If the desired cards were together, the first one the eighth from the top, and the others the next two cards, the count would stand eight, one, one.

The calculation of the positions the cards will take when thrown on the deck is made before the dealer gathers them up to shuffle, or as he is doing so. It is a very simple matter to note the order in which two or three desirable cards lie, or, for that matter, five or six. In some games the note is made as the tricks are taken. In others the last cards that are faced on the table give sufficient choice. For instance, if two hands are shown in a Poker game, one holding a small pair and the other a side card to match the pair, a glance would determine the order the Three of a Kind would take when thrown on the deck. Of course, it would not do to make up the desired cards from one hand. Lightning don't strike in the same place often, and the dealer would naturally feel a little diffident about holding the same good cards that were contained in the last hand shown. The Cull Shuffle will bring the desired cards to the bottom of the deck. As a first example we will cull two desired cards.

To Cull Two Cards, Numbers 8, 4. — Under-cut about half deck, in-jog first card and shuffle off. Under-cut to in-jog, run one less than first number, in-jog, running one more than second number, out-jog and shuffle off. (The two desired cards are now located at top and bottom of the middle packet, which is held by the in- and out-jogs.) Under-cut to out-jog, forming break at in-jog, in-jog first card (a desired card), throw to break, and shuffle off. (The two desired cards are now together, being the in-jog card and the next above it.) Under-cut to in-jog and shuffle off. This leaves the two desired cards at the bottom.

The action is a little confusing at first, but when this system of culling is understood it becomes very simple. The first under-cut and shuffle off, in the foregoing example, has no bearing on the result, but it places the cards to be worked on well down in the deck, and this aids in making the whole shuffle appear regular.

To Cull Three Cards, Numbers 7, 5, 9. — Under-cut about half deck, in-jog first card and shuffle off. Under-cut to in-jog, run one less than first number, in-jog running one more than second number, out-jog running one less than third number, and throw on top. (Two of the desired cards are now at top and bottom of middle packet and the third on top of the deck.) Under-cut to out-jog, forming break at in-jog, in-jog top card, run one, throw to break and shuffle off. (The three cards are now together at in-jog.) Under-cut to in-jog, and shuffle off, leaving the three desired cards at the bottom.

It is necessary to put some little brains into so simple a problem as adding two and two together, and to become accomplished at culling one must have an understanding of the cause and effect of the various actions. It is impossible to give a formula that will answer for every situation. There is no end to the variety of positions the desired cards may be in. But with a thorough knowledge of the two examples given, and the reason for each particular action, the student will be fairly established on the road to success, and have overcome by far the greatest difficulty.

To Cull Four Cards, Numbers 3, 6, 2, 5. — Under-cut about one-third deck, in-jog first card and shuffle off. Under-cut to in-jog, run one less than first number, in-jog running one more than second number, out-jog running one less than third number, and throw on top. (Two of the cards are now at top and bottom of middle packet, one on top of deck, and the last at its original number from top card.) Under-cut to out-jog, forming break at in-jog, in-jog top card, run one, throw to break and shuffle off. (Three cards are now together at in-jog, and last card at its number below in-jog.) Under-cut to in-jog and run one less than last number and throw on top. (Three of the cards are now at the bottom, the fourth on top.)

The top card can now be brought to the bottom with its fellows by an under-cut to top card and a throw on top; or, under-cut about half deck, in-jog top card, and throw on top; then under-cut to in-jog and shuffle off.

To under-cut to top card and throw on top, or, in other words, to run one and throw balance on top, if done rapidly, appears like a simple cut, and the fact that but one card is taken from the top to the bottom cannot be detected.

These examples of culling, if fairly well executed, have all the appearance of an ordinary shuffle, and when performed with the smoothness and grace of a clever card handler it is absolutely impossible to detect the least manipulation.

It will be noticed in the examples given that culling is largely a repetition of the same actions, as the number to be culled increases; and consequently the time required is greater. But should the desired cards run together in pairs, as threes or more, the action and time are shortened proportionately. Sets of cards running together are treated much as though each set were one card. If the order be 6, 1, 1, 1, 4, 1, 1, the action of getting them all together will be much the same as though they were but two cards at 6, 4. If the order were 5, 1, 1, 1, 3, 1, 1, 7, 1, the action would be about the same as a three-card cull shuffle, though there are nine desired cards actually run down to the bottom.

To Cull Nine Cards, Numbers 5, 1, 1, 1, 3, 1, 1, 7, 1. — Under-cut about one-third deck, in-jog first card and shuffle off. Under-cut to in-jog and run one less than first number, in-jog running all cards to and including last card of second set. (This run is nine, four in first set, two indifferent cards, three in second set.) Out-jog running one less than next number (six), and throw on top. (This places first two sets at top and bottom of middle packet, and third set on top.) Under-cut to out-jog, forming break at in-jog, in-jog top card, run second set (three), throw to break and shuffle off. (All the desired cards are now together, but the in-jog divides the last two.) Under-cut to in-jog and throw on top. This leaves one card on top and eight on bottom.

This example might well be termed a fancy cull, as running down so many cards will rarely be attempted, but it shows the possibilities of the system. Before the shuffle is begun the entire action should be mentally rehearsed so that there will be no hesitation in the procedure.

There is no difficult sleight-of-hand manipulation connected with the operation. Any one who can shuffle can cull, if he has the understanding. Rapidity is not nearly so important as regularity of time and movement.

There are many ways of making the cull shuffle more simple. The dealer can gather up the cards with a great deal of judgment yet without apparent design. He will never face a card or cards, or never change the positions in any group, but he can pick up any card or group of cards in the order best suited to his design without attracting attention. He can note the order the cards fall, in any particular trick, how many cards or tricks have been thrown on top of those he desires, the order of any discard exposed, his own discard, and the last cards played on the table. There are scores of opportunities to note the order of desirable cards in any game. If the dealer has an ally the two may work together in gathering up the cards, and the possibilities are doubled.

When the desired cards are run down to the bottom the dealer could continue the shuffle and run up a top stock, but the time required for the two operations would be too long. The usual practice is to deal from the bottom. Fifteen or twenty seconds is plenty of time to execute a three-card cull shuffle, and it can be done in half the time.

ERDNASE SYSTEM OF PALMING

The art of card palming can be brought to a degree of perfection that borders on the wonderful. It is very simple to place one or several cards in the palm and conceal them by partly closing and turning the palm downward, or inward; but it is entirely another matter to palm them from the deck in such a manner that the most critical observer would not even suspect, let alone detect, the action. The methods following were originated by us, and we believe them to be the most rapid and subtle ever devised.

TOP PALM. *First Method.* — Hold the deck in the left hand so that the first joints of the second and third fingers will be against the middle of one side, the thumb against middle of opposite side, the first joint of little finger against middle of end and first finger curled up against bottom. Bring the right hand over top of deck, the third, second and little fingers close together, first joint of the little finger being against the end corner, the first finger curled up on top and the tip of thumb resting idly at end, above left little finger. To palm, press the right little finger, exactly at the first joint, firmly against the top cards, pull them up about half an inch at corner, freeing them from the left second and third fingers, keeping the three right fingers (little, second and third) perfectly straight. The cards to be palmed are now held firmly between the right little finger, and the left little finger. (See Fig. 36.) Straighten out right

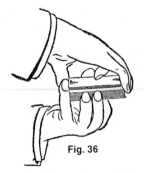

Fig. 36

first finger, swing left little finger with the cards to be palmed free of the end of the deck, press the cards into the right palm with the end of the left third finger. (See Fig. 37.) Draw the deck out about half way from

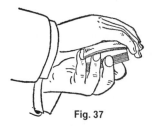

Fig. 37

under the right hand, and release the left hand entirely. (See Fig. 38.) Then the right drops the deck on the table to be cut. After the hands are in the first position the whole process does not occupy half a second.

The deck should be kept in view as much as possible, and the right first finger is curled up on top for that purpose until the instant the palm is performed. The action of drawing the deck into view when the cards are palmed is made a part of the whole movement.

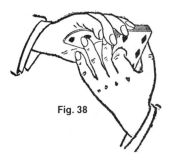

Fig. 38

TOP PALM. *Second Method.* — The positions of the hands are identically the same as the first method, a slight difference is made in the process of palming. Pull up the cards to be palmed as before, then insert the ends of the left second and third fingers. Now straighten out right first finger, press down on end of deck with all four right fingers, bending the cards to be palmed over the left second and third finger ends, and holding them in place by left little finger. Release left little finger and the cards will spring up into the right palm, the left second finger aiding the movement by pressing the cards firmly into the palm and holding them there while the deck is being drawn into view by the left hand. As described in the former method, the left hand should immediately release the deck, which is dropped on the table by the right.

We consider these methods the best for palming the top cards after a shuffle. The positions the hands assume are taken quite naturally in squaring up the cards. The right hand should seize the ends first, and the left thumb and fingers square up the sides by sliding up and down; then by moving the left little finger to the end of deck the proper position is obtained and the palm made in a twinkling.

When the cut is made reach the right hand boldly for the deck, but instead of picking it up lay the palmed cards on top and draw the deck to the edge of the table. Then the thumb naturally goes under the end and the cards can be picked up with ease.

BOTTOM PALM. *First Method.* — Seize the deck with the right hand on top, between the first joints of the second and third fingers at one end, and the thumb at the other end; the fingers close together and the third finger and thumb close to each corner so as to expose as much of the deck as possible. Bring up the left hand and seize the deck from beneath at the right thumb end, between the first and second fingers, and the palm just under the second joint of the thumb, the thumb lying straight across the top close to the end. If this position is secured correctly the tips of the left thumb and second finger touch the right thumb, as all three are at the same corner of the deck and almost the whole of the deck is exposed. To palm, grip the bottom cards at the side of corner with the tip of the left second finger, squeezing them in against the palm under the left thumb, and pull down over end of right thumb about a quarter of an inch. (See Fig. 39.) This will cause the outer-end corner of the under cards to project a little at the side, under the right

Fig. 39

third finger. Catch the projecting corner with the right little fingertip, pressing the cards firmly against palm under the left thumb, and draw them in toward right thumb, — at the same time straightening out the left fingers — until the under cards lie fairly along the left palm. (See Fig. 40.) Slightly close left hand with the palmed cards and turn partly over and inward as the right hand lays the deck on the table for the cut.

The entire action of this palm is extremely rapid, simple, easy and imperceptible. The only difficulty is in establishing the proper position for the left hand. To get this absolutely exact, palm half a dozen cards in the left hand in the most favorable position for holding and concealing.

Fig. 40

Then with one finger of the right hand press against the little finger corner of the palmed cards, and — using the diagonal corner as a pivot — swing them out and over the first finger until the left second fingertip can be brought against the corner, and the left thumb lies across the end. Now, if the left thumb is raised and the balance of the deck is placed on top, the desired position is obtained.

After a shuffle, the position is taken quite naturally in squaring up by merely pushing the deck out of the left palm until the left thumb lies along the top close to the end.

This palm may be made without the aid of the right little finger. The positions of the hands are taken exactly as before, then the second left finger is dropped sufficiently to allow the little finger to take its place. The little finger then grips the corner and pulls the cards back to the left wrist until they lie along the left fingers as before.

BOTTOM PALM. *Second Method.* — Seize the deck with the right hand on top, by the middle of the ends between the thumb and first joints of second and third fingers, first finger curled up on top. Bring the left hand up against the bottom, the left second and third finger tips resting idly on the right second and third fingers, the left little finger at first joint against the edge of the bottom cards at the same end, the left first finger curled up against bottom and the left thumb resting against the side. To palm, grip the corner of the under cards with the left little finger at first joint. (See Fig. 41.) Then swing finger end of upper portion of deck out against left thumb, keeping right thumb stationary as a pivot, until the finger ends of the two packets are just past each other, straightening out the left first finger at the same time. (See Fig. 42.) Then release thumb end of lower packet, letting it down into left palm, or press thumb end of both packets into left palm, releasing under packet, and slide deck out of left hand and drop it on the table to be cut, turning over left hand with the palmed cards at the same moment.

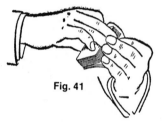

Fig. 41

The whole process is as quick as a flash, and quite imperceptible. The drawback is the slightly unnatural action of bringing the left fingers to the end of the deck. They should be kept at the side in squaring up after

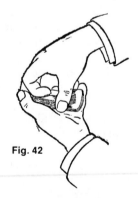

Fig. 42

the shuffle, then at the last instant slipped to the end, and without a moment's hesitation the palm is made.

To replace the bottom palm, pick up the deck by the ends with the right hand, and as it is placed in the left slide the left second finger from the end of the palmed cards to the side, curl the left first finger up underneath (see Fig. 43), and as the palmed cards are slipped into position bring the left thumb against one side and the left second finger to the other, which materially aid in the rotary movement of the under packet.

It is more difficult to replace than to palm, but the action is not so liable to attract attention, as, if the palm is not suspected, any awkwardness at replacing may be covered by squaring up the cut. But replacing may be performed just as perfectly as palming, and to become

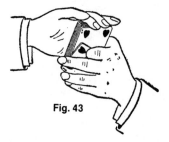

Fig. 43

proficient in either requires some practice. When the positions and process are thoroughly understood the main difficulties are overcome.

BOTTOM PALM. *When Cards Are Riffled.* — When the cards are riffled — that is, shuffled on the table — it is impossible to make a palm in a perfectly natural manner, as there is no reason for taking the deck up into the hands before the cut. The action would appear awkward, or at least unnecessary and a waste of time. But when the company is not too fast the following plan may be used with success.

After the riffle seize the deck at sides, near ends, between second finger and thumb of each hand. Raise the left-hand end until the bottom card faces the left palm, and give the deck a gentle tap on its end on the table. (See Fig. 44.) Then release the right hand and tilt the deck

Fig. 44

outward, so that the right second finger and thumb can grasp the ends near the top corners. Now release the left fingers, retaining position of left thumb, and tap the table again with the side of deck, at the same time bringing left second and third fingers to end of deck and curling left first and little fingers against the bottom, the left third finger touching the table. (See Fig. 45.) This brings the hands into much the same position as the "Second Method." To palm, grip the bottom cards with the

Fig. 45

left third finger at first joint, and press firmly against right thumb; raise whole deck slightly, swinging finger end of top portion against left thumb, keeping right thumb stationary as a pivot, until the finger ends of both packets are past each other, and straightening out left first and little fingers. (See Fig. 46.) Then press right thumb with ends of both packets down into left palm, releasing under packet, and slide the deck out of left hand to be cut, turning over the left with the palmed ends at the same time.

After the deck is on its side the movements are perfectly natural in appearance, and the action of tapping the edges on the table to square up is common enough to pass in most any company. But tipping the deck may give an opportunity to note the bottom card, and the action will more likely cause a suspicion of that design than of palming. However, the tilting and tapping may be accomplished without haste and in a manner plainly evident that no one can possibly get a glimpse.

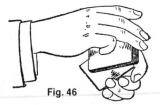

Fig. 46

The left hand should completely cover the bottom card, and the deck so handled that at no time does it face either the dealer or the players.

The actual palming can be done in a flash, and as we have said, the only objections are the necessary manœuvers to obtain the position in a natural and easy manner.

The top palm can be made with the right hand in much the same manner, by reversing the positions. In which case the right hand seizes the deck by the sides after the palm is made. But there is little occasion for top palming in any game. In the second part of this book will be found, under the caption "Changes," several methods of palming which are lightning-like in rapidity but are more applicable to card conjuring than card playing.

TO MAINTAIN THE BOTTOM PALM
WHILE DEALING

The bottom palm may be held while the deal is in progress without inconvenience. The ruse is adopted for one of several reasons. It may be to avoid the risk of replacing the palm immediately after the cut; as a more favorable opportunity occurs just after the deal when the remainder of the deck is placed on the table. This would be of service in games

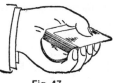

Fig. 47

such as Poker or Casino. The bottom cards can be obtained on the second deal. Sometimes the palm is made after the cut and maintained throughout the deal for the purpose of holding too many. The dealer's cards are placed on the palmed cards, the whole "skinned" through, the discard palmed again in one or the other hand, and replaced when the deck is taken up again. If the bottom palm is made before the cut and maintained throughout the deal it both gives too many and avoids the necessity of bottom dealing, but it is a very poor substitute. This is fully explained under caption of "Skinning the Hand."

The cards are palmed in the left hand and the deck placed across them. The deal is begun immediately. The four fingers of the left hand are kept close together with the tips held firmly against the side of deck, and effectually conceal the palmed cards. (See Fig. 47.) There is little or no difficulty in performing this perfectly, and the deal can be carried on without a sign to indicate the manœuver. The palmed cards will be crimped from their position and the warmth of the hand. The crimp must be taken out when squaring up.

TO HOLD THE LOCATION OF CUT WHILE DEALING

The object of holding the location of the cut is so that a shift may be made at that point when the first deal has been completed. This will bring the original bottom cards to that position again, from which they may be dealt during the second deal, and the most opportune moment for the shift is immediately after the first deal, as the deck is deposited on the table.

When the cut is made, pick up the packet that was under, by the sides, near end, between second and third fingers and thumb of right hand, and lay it on top of packet cut-off, so that the then under packet forms a jog or protrudes about quarter of an inch toward the right wrist. Pick up the two packets the instant the one is placed on the other, by a sliding movement, with the fingers in the same position, and place the deck across the left palm with the left thumb on top to hold it in position. Then release sides of deck with right hand and seize ends to square up. In doing so the right thumb comes against the inner end and in contact with the jog or projecting under packet. Press this down a little with the thumb and square ends of deck, forming break at thumb end. Now shift the left hand slightly so as to hold the break with the tip of the left little finger at the side, close to the end, and begin the deal. (See Fig. 48.) The break is not more than an eighth of an inch wide, and is concealed by the left third finger. The action is very simple, yet should be carefully studied. The slight jog in the two packets as they are picked up is not noticeable, as the top packet overhangs at the outer end and the one most likely to show is hidden by the right hand. But in any case it would not matter much, as the action of squaring up after the deck is placed in the left palm appears genuine, and the break can be formed without a possibility of detection. The little finger can hold the break by pressing

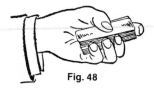

Fig. 48

against the ball of the thumb without the least inconvenience while the deal progresses.

SHIFTS

There are many methods of performing the manœuver that reverses the action of the cut, but in this part of our work we will describe but three which we consider at all practicable at the card table. This artifice is erroneously supposed to be indispensable to the professional player, but the truth is it is little used, and adopted only as a last resort. The conjurer employs the shift in nine-tenths of his card tricks, and under his environments it is comparatively very simple to perform. A half turn of the body, or a slight swing of the hands, or the use of "patter" until a favorable moment occurs, enables him to cover the action perfectly. But seated at the card table in a money game, the conditions are different. The hands may not be withdrawn from the table for an instant, and any unusual swing or turn will not be tolerated, and a still greater handicap arises

Fig. 49

from the fact that the object of a shift is well known, and especially the exact moment to expect it, immediately after the cut. The shift has yet to be invented that can be executed by a movement appearing as coincident card-table routine; or that can be executed with the hands held stationary and not show that some manœuver has taken place, however cleverly it may be performed. Nevertheless upon occasion it must be employed, and the resourceful professional failing to improve the method changes the moment; and by this expedient overcomes the principal obstacle in the way of accomplishing the action unobserved.

This subterfuge is explained in our treatment of the subject, "The Player Without an Ally," under the distinctive heading, "Shifting the Cut."

The first shift described is executed with both hands and is a great favorite. It is probably the oldest and best in general use.

TWO-HANDED SHIFT. — Hold the deck in the left hand, the thumb on one side, the first, second and third fingers curled around the other side with the first joints pressing against the top of the deck and the little

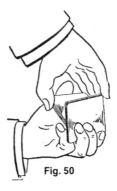

Fig. 50

finger inserted at the cut, or between the two packets that are to be reversed. The deck is held slantingly, with the right side downward. Bring up the right hand and cover the deck, seizing the lower packet by the ends between the thumb and second finger, about half an inch from the upper corners, the right-hand fingers being close together but none of them touching the deck but the thumb and second finger. (See Fig. 49.) If this position is properly taken the right hand holds the lower packet and the left hand clips the upper packet between the little finger and the other three. Now, to reverse the position of the two packets, the right hand holds the lower packet firmly against the left thumb, and the left fingers draw off the upper packet, under cover of the right hand (see Fig. 50), so that it just clears the side of the lower packet, and then swing it in underneath. (See Fig. 51.) The left thumb aids the two packets to clear each other by pressing down on the side of the under packet, so as to tilt up the opposite side as the upper packet is drawn off. The under packet being held by only one finger and thumb, can be tilted as though it worked on a swivel at each end, and the right fingers may retain their relative positions throughout. Most teachers advise assisting the action by having the fingers of the right hand pull up on the lower packet, but we believe the blind is much more perfect if there is not the least change

Fig. 51

in the attitude of the right fingers during or immediately after the shift. The packets can be reversed like a flash, and without the least noise, but it requires considerable practice to accomplish the feat perfectly. The positions must be accurately secured and the action performed slowly until accustomed to the movements.

ERDNASE SHIFT. *One Hand.* — The following method is the outcome of persistent effort to devise a shift that may be employed with the greatest probability of success at the card table. It is vastly superior for this purpose, because the action takes place before the right hand seizes the deck, and just as it is about to do so, thereby covering naturally and actually performing the work before the action is anticipated. It is extremely rapid and noiseless, and the two packets pass through the least possible space in changing their position. The drawback is the extreme difficulty in mastering it perfectly. Many hours of incessant practice must be spent to acquire the requisite amount of skill; but it must be remembered if feats at card-handling could be attained for the asking there would be little in such performance to interest or profit any one.

Hold the deck in the left hand, little finger at one end, first and second fingers at side, thumb diagonally across top of deck with first joint pressed down against the opposite end, and the third finger curled up against the bottom. The second fingertip holds a break at the side, locating the cut, or separating the two packets that are to be reversed. (See Fig. 52.) Now, by squeezing the under packet between the second finger and palm and pressing the upper packet with the thumb at one end against the little finger at the other end, it will be found that the two packets can be moved independently. To reverse their positions, hold the upper packet firmly by pressing with the thumb, open the two packets at the break and draw out the under packet with the second and third fingers, the second finger pulling down and third finger pressing up, until the inner side of the under packet just clears the outside of the

Fig. 52

upper packet. (See Fig. 53.) Then press the lower packet up and over on top. When getting the under packet out and forcing it clear of the upper packet, it is turned a little by the third finger, so that the corner at the little finger end appears over the side first. The little finger aids in getting the under packet over or the upper packet underneath by pull-

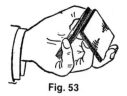

Fig. 53

ing down on the upper packet when the lower one is just appearing over the side. (See Fig. 54.)

Doubtless the first attempts to make this shift will impress the student that it is impossible. The very unusual positions of the fingers will appear to give them no control over the deck; but the facts are the packets may be held with vice-like rigidity during the entire operation, or it may be performed by holding the packets very loosely, and in each case either in a twinkling or very slowly.

The principal difficulty will be in drawing out the under packet in such a manner that it will not fly out of the fingers. It must not spring away from the upper packet at all, but should slip along, up, and over in one continuous movement.

Of course, in performing this shift at the card table the right hand is brought over the deck just at the moment of action, and the operation may be greatly facilitated by allowing the under packet to spring very lightly against the right palm; but the finished performer will use the

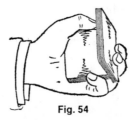

Fig. 54

right hand only as a cover, and it will take no part at all in the action. We presume that the larger, or the longer hand, the easier it will be for a beginner to accomplish this shift, but a very small hand can perform the action when the knack is once acquired.

The amateur who does not wish to spend the time necessary to perfect himself in this very difficult one-handed shift, may obtain nearly the same result by adopting the following method, which is performed with both hands and is very much easier:

ERDNASE SHIFT. *Two Hands.* — Hold the deck in the left hand as described in the one-hand shift, except that the first finger is curled up against the bottom and the third finger is held against the side. Now bring the right hand over the deck, the fingers held close together but in easy position, and insert the tip of the little finger in the break at side close to outer corner, just sufficiently to press down on corner of the under packet. To make the shift, press down with the right little finger, and out and up with the left first finger, holding the upper packet firmly between left thumb and little finger. (See Fig. 55.) The lower packet will

Fig. 55

spring into the right palm, the top packet is lowered by the left thumb and little finger, and the bottom packet closed in on top by the left second and third fingers. This two-handed form of the shift is comparatively very easy to execute; it is extremely rapid and can be performed without the least noise.

TO ASCERTAIN THE TOP CARDS WHILE RIFFLING AND RESERVE THEM AT BOTTOM

During the process of a riffle an expert performer can obtain a glimpse of the top cards and bring them to the bottom in reserve for the deal. It requires a suspicious and very knowing player to detect the ruse. The glimpse is obtained by slightly in-jogging the top card of the left-hand packet, as explained in treatment of "Blind Riffles," under caption, "No. I To Retain Top Stock." As the thumbs raise the corners of the two packets to riffle, the top card is slightly jogged over and raised by the left

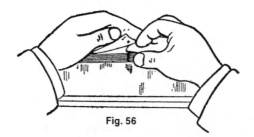

Fig. 56

thumb, just barely enough to obtain a glance at the index, and when the cards are riffled the card seen is left on top, as it naturally should be. (See Fig. 56.) It is quite possible to get a glimpse without jogging the card if the cards are sprung in the usual manner and the last one retained for an instant in a slightly elevated position by the left thumb. But this operation is more liable of detection. The opportune moment, both to jog and to get the glimpse, is after the corners are raised and as the thumbs are about to release the cards. The top card is brought to the bottom by a ruse worked in connection with the Blind Cut, described under heading of "No. IV To Retain Bottom Stock." An under-cut is made with the right hand, and as the packet is placed on top it is done with a sidling movement, the tip of the right thumb lightly slides across the top card of the then under packet, pushing it a little over the inner side. The left thumb is at the side to receive it, and forms a break, so that it becomes the under card of the top packet when squared up. Then the Blind Cut is executed as described, the top packet to the break is drawn off first, and the rest of the deck in several packets, and the particular card is left at the bottom. The riffle is again executed, retaining this card at the bottom, the glimpse obtained of the next top card of the left-hand packet, which is brought down in like manner, and so on. These cards might be left on top, but they would be of little use there. If at the bottom, the knowledge of two or three cards is of immense advantage to an expert. When playing alone he either deals without replacing on the cut, or palms for the cut, or shifts after the cut. If he has an ally on his right a Blind Cut is made. In any case he deals the cards from the bottom, to himself if they are desirable, and to an opponent if not.

MODE OF HOLDING THE HAND

The professional player, ever conscious of the necessity of uniformity, will always hold his hand in the same manner; and as he often finds it convenient to have more than his share of the cards, the position must be one which will always disguise that possibility. The best for all purposes is as follows:

Hold the cards in the left hand, the end fitting into the third joints of the first, second and third fingers, the lower corner resting on the little finger close to the third joint, and the little finger curled in so that the cards rest on the first joint also. The left thumb rests on the upper side, and the first, second and third fingers are curled in so that their tips rest against the back.

To read the cards, bring the right hand up, the third finger against the under side, the little finger against the end, the first and second fingers curled up on back, and the thumb on top. (See Fig. 57.) Then, with a sliding downward movement of the left thumb crimp or convex the cards sufficiently to read the index on each; or, open the edges slightly with the right thumb by springing the cards one at a time against the left

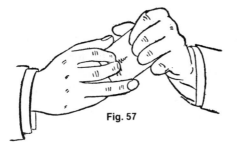

Fig. 57

thumb, which is pressed on top to keep them open. This exact position is very important for several reasons, principally because it effectually conceals the number held, and it enables the player to "skin" his hand and palm off the extra cards without fuss or unusual movements. In general appearance the hold is the same as adopted by very many players for the excellent purpose of preventing bystanders from getting a glimpse.

SKINNING THE HAND

When too many cards are held the hand must be sorted, the extra cards brought to top or bottom, the discard palmed and restored, smoothly, rapidly and with movements that are customary.

The cards are held as described for "Mode of Holding the Hand." Separate the upper edges with both thumbs so that the right thumb can press against the card to be brought to the top. Bend this card slightly between right thumb and second and third fingers, so that it can be slipped from

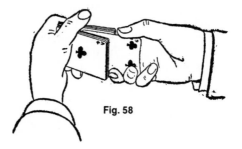

Fig. 58

beneath the left thumb. Then, holding this card firmly, and keeping the right hand almost stationary, pull out the rest of the cards with the left hand by a backward and inward motion and by pressing the left finger-tips against the back. (See Fig. 58.) Then shove the right-hand card on top. The action is not concealed, but made openly. It is a very common procedure for arranging any hand for play or discard. If the discard happen to lie together, bring them to the top with one action.

Now the top cards must be palmed, and one of the methods already described in this work may be employed. But for use in this particular case we would advise another palm, which is most fitting for a discard, and especially the movements leading up to the actual palming. Form a break between the discard and the rest and hold the break with the right thumb. Shift the left thumb to the outer-end corner of the under packet, and slide it down about half an inch into the right palm. Close the break, hold cards with left hand, release the right and push the cards further down into the right palm between base of thumb and third and little fingers, sufficiently to allow tips of right thumb and second finger

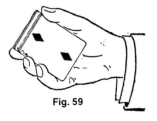

Fig. 59

to reach the outer-end corners over the left thumb and little finger. (See Fig. 59.) Now release the left hand entirely and turn the right palm downward. This position covers the sides and the inner end completely, concealing the quantity, and the fact that the packets overlap, and yet has a very easy and natural appearance. (See Fig. 60.) The right hand can now nonchalantly hold the cards, while the left handles the chips or makes a bet. When ready to deal again, the left hand seizes the cards from below, at the middle of sides, between second and third fingers and thumb, and the little finger on the protruding corner of the under packet, and at the same moment the right four fingers are shifted to the outer end as if to take the fresh hold. Press down on the outer end, hold inner protruding end with left little finger, release the upper packet which is held by the left thumb and second and third fingers (see

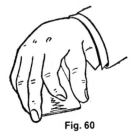

Fig. 60

Fig. 61), and it will spring up into the right palm. The left hand instantly draws the under packet out sideways about half way, and the right hand drops it on the table and then places the palmed cards on the deck while

Fig. 61

picking it up. This method of palming is excellent after the position is secured, and under the circumstances just described it is better to take this position than to make the palm immediately after the hand is skinned. If it is desired to palm in the left hand, the discard is retained and the others brought to the top while skinning. Then one of the bottom palms described must be employed.

THE PLAYER WITHOUT AN ALLY

It is the general belief that it takes two to obtain any advantage in a card game with knowing players — the dealer and the man who cuts. That this is generally true cannot be denied, but it is by no means always so. There are many ways of beating the game alone, and though the percentage in favor of the single player may be less in any given instance, it is pretty constant and quite sufficient to insure a very comfortable living to many clever people, though the card table is their sole source of revenue.

The greatest obstacle in the path of the lone player is the cut. It is the bête noire of his existence. Were it not for this formality his deal would mean the money. Though he may run up a hand however cleverly, the cut sends him to sea again. "Put your faith in Providence, but always cut the cards," is a wise injunction. Sometimes the cut is not made, and the adept dearly loves to sit on the left of a player who is careless enough to occasionally say, "Run them" — i. e., he waives the cut. Professional players always calculate on such a possibility, and will continue to stock on every deal to some extent with that chance in view.

Dealing Without the Cut. — When the dealer has desired cards on the bottom and the cut is made without replacing the two packets, he will pick up the packet that was under and immediately proceed to deal from that alone. In this way he can get the under cards by bottom dealing. The cut is usually made in this way, and the dealer aids the play by being ready to seize the under packet as the top is lifted off. However, if the company will not stand for this, and some one says, "Carry the cut," he will, of course, do so in future and turn his attention to other manœuvres.

Replacing the Cut as Before. — A daring and yet oftentimes successful ruse of overcoming the cut difficulty is to pick up the under packet with the right hand, and instead of placing it on the other packet it is slid across the table into the left hand, and then the second packet placed on top in the same way. The packets may be picked up by the right hand instead of sliding them. The move is made quite openly, carelessly and without haste, and is surprisingly regular in appearance. It will not pass in fast company, but the beauty of it is that if noticed it can be attributed to thoughtlessness.

Holding Out for the Cut. — To hold out in a card game is the riskiest and most dangerous form of taking advantage that a player may attempt, but it can be, and is, successfully practiced when cleverly performed and the player is not suspected. But the only hold out that we consider really safe is made by the dealer, and but for the moment of cutting. After a blind shuffle, with the desired cards on the bottom, the dealer palms in the left and passes the deck with the right to be cut. After the cut he picks up the deck with the right hand and replaces the palmed cards when squaring up for the deal. Of course, this necessitates a perfect knowledge of palming and replacing, but both actions then become possible in any kind of company, if the player is not suspected. Holding out for the cut is incomparably less risky than holding out on another's deal; as the deck is never subject to being handled or counted, and the palmed cards remain in the dealer's possession but for the moment.

When there are but two or three players in a game where the cards are dealt one at a time, a top stock of four or six cards may be run up and palmed in the right hand as the deck is passed for the cut. The top palm is replaced when picking up the deck, and usually by a sliding motion. This palming and replacing of the top stock is easier and perhaps less noticeable, and does not require the bottom work in the deal; but when there are five or six players, or when the cards are dealt two or more at a time, the quantity to be palmed would be too bulky.

Shifting the Cut. — There is a current supposition that the expert player employs what is commonly known as the two-handed shift to reverse the action of the cut, but there has never been a shift invented that can be executed during a card game by movements that appear quite regular. If the professional player could always sit in with neophytes, who would stand for actions that are foreign to the usual procedure, he would have little need of special ability to get the money. In the average game where the players keep their hands, and arms also, on the table there is little opportunity to shift the cut. Still there is an opportune moment in some games when the shift may be made with probabilities of being unnoticed. It is immediately after the first deal. The dealer holds the location of the cut until the hands are dealt, and makes the shift as he lays down the deck. Then the desired cards can be dealt from the bottom during the next deal. This moment, after the first deal, is the most favorable, as the players are occupied with their hands, the cut has been made quite regularly, the deal finished and consequently there is less cause for close scrutiny. But principally because the shift can be made with a much more natural action when about to lay down the deck than when picking it up, and also because the deck is much smaller after the deal and therefore so much easier to shift. In any game where cards are dealt the second time the play holds good. But, in any event, shifting is much more noticeable than palming for the cut.

Dealing Too Many. — A favorable and perhaps the most generally used advantage is in the dealer giving himself one or two extra cards on the last round. The quantity is not noticeable when lying on the table, and as the extra cards are taken on the last round there is little time for inspection. The dealer immediately picks them up with the left hand as the deck is deposited on the table by the right. The selection is made and the discard palmed and gotten rid of as described under headline, "Skinning the Hand." When holding too many in Poker, it is preferable to palm and replace the extra cards on the deck when picking it up to deal the draw than to make the discard and throw the extra cards with it on the discard heap. The dealer palms the extra cards, lays his full hand on the table, replaces the palmed cards, deals the draw and his own draw, then makes his discard and picks up his draw.

A second method of taking too many is by palming the desired number after the deal. The left hand makes the palm as the right is about to lay down the deck. A still safer plan is to make the palm immediately after the cut when squaring up, and maintain the palm while dealing. This can be done perfectly and avoids the slightest hesitation or movement after the deal is finished.

Crimping for the Cut. — The probability of the unsuspecting player cutting into a crimp is always kept in view. The process of crimping is fully explained under caption "To Indicate the Location for the Cut." When crimping for the chance of the cut being made at that point, the bend is put in more forcibly, and sometimes if the company is not too fast, the two packets may be crimped in opposite directions, creating quite a space and thereby increasing the probabilities of the player unconsciously cutting into it. The packets may be crimped concave, or convex, as thought best for the player's mode of cutting, but the deck should be squared up perfectly and laid down accordingly. It is the rule for players to cut in about the same manner each time. That is, he cuts high, low or near the middle, and seizes the cards by the sides or ends. The mode of cutting oftentimes becomes a habit that is unconsciously followed. The observant dealer is thus enabled to put in his crimp high or low, in about the location most favorable, and concave if the player cuts by the ends, and convex if at the sides. The deck must be laid down so that the hand which the player habitually uses will come naturally into the most favorable position to oblige the dealer. Even if the crimp is missed it still locates the stock, and the dealer has other opportunities of profiting thereby. Of course crimped cards are never dealt. The crimp is effectually taken out by bending in the opposite direction.

Replacing Palm When Cutting. — As a general rule the card expert will not hold out except on his own deal for the cut; however, we shall describe an exception that is at times worked successfully. The player on the dealer's right may hold out a palm in either hand, and replace it when given the deck to cut. In games wherein the whole deck is dealt, the hold out is usually palmed in the right hand back to palm. When the deck is received he makes a running cut, seizing the deck by the ends in both hands. The first pass to take of the first small packet, is a blind, and the palmed cards are dropped on the table. Precisely the same movement is made as in taking off a small packet by the ends. Then the running cut is continued, leaving the palmed cards on the bottom.

Another method is to palm in the left hand face to palm. The cut is made with the right hand, and then the deck placed in the left on the palmed cards, the replacing appearing as a square up. But this plan is risky, as there is little excuse for squaring upon another's deal. If a one-handed fancy cut is made with the right hand, and the cards left somewhat scattered, they may be with more propriety, taken up into both hands and squared.

A third way, and the most generally employed, is for the right hand holding the palmed cards back to palm to make a cut by the ends, and then deposit the palmed cards on the packet that was under, when picking it up to put in place. This is good in any game as the palmed cards are dealt first.

Cleverly executed, a holdout can be replaced in cutting without attracting the least notice, but it requires as much practice and study as any other artifice. As the player who cuts was the last dealer, it usually gives him a good opportunity to hold out and arrange desired cards; and as such an advantage is on another's deal, it greatly increases the percentages of the expert. The methods described can be successfully worked with as many as eight or ten cards, though of course the greater the number, the more probability of the dealer noticing the diminished condition of the deck; but it requires a good judge to detect the absence of half a dozen or so. Of course cards so held out to replace when cutting are arranged so that the desirable cards will fall to the operator.

The cautious and prudent expert makes it a rule to never "hold out," or palm extra cards, or deal himself too many, or obtain more than his share through any artifice, unless the regular procedure of the game will bring the deck into his possession, so that he can get rid of the extra quantity, naturally and easily, by replacing them on the top or bottom of the pack. To "go south" with extra cards, i. e., to drop them in the lap, or conceal them any place about the person, or hold them palmed during the play, or even to throw them on the discard heap when making his own discard, is inartistic, and risky, and unworthy of any but a neophyte or a bungler. Possibly the most closely watched procedure, and the easiest to observe in a Poker game, is the number of cards that are discarded; and where there is the least suspicion, discarding too many in the ordinary way is surely detected. When playing Poker the expert will hold too many only on his own deal, and then only before the draw. He can palm and replace the extra card or cards when about to deal the draw.

In Cribbage the non-dealer may hold out one or two cards, and after the crib is laid out, replace the extra card when cutting for the turn-up. But in whatsoever game, where cards are held out at all, the rule holds good that they must be restored, and at a moment when the regular procedure of the game necessitates the handling of the deck.

Cassino gives the dealer many opportunities of holding too many, as the deck is continuously handled during the game.

The Short Deck. — A simple method of obtaining an advantage in many games is that of playing with a "short" deck. Several cards are removed entirely from the pack, but retained in the memory, and the game is played without them. The knowledge that these particular cards are withheld enables the strategist to make his calculations and play his own cards with a great deal more certainty. Cards held out entirely are usually destroyed, or otherwise effectually disposed of, so as to preclude the possibility of the schemer being discovered "with the goods on him." A very bold expedient at Two-Handed Cassino is to dispose of eight cards. This runs the deck to five deals instead of six. The lower cards are usually selected, and of different denominations, say the Four and Six of Spades, and the Deuce, Tray, Four, Five, Seven and Eight of other suits. With this arrangement, or depletion, an adversary enjoying ordinary luck, will find in summing up his points that he does not make "cards" or "Spades" in a very long time indeed, and of course he credits his opponent with three points. The idea of so many cards being withheld from the deck without being noticed, will doubtless cause certain Cassino players to smile. We don't think many shrewd players could be so imposed upon, but we regret the truth of the confession that once upon a time we were, and we marveled greatly and also sorrowed, over a continuous and very protracted run of "hard luck."

THREE CARD MONTE

We cannot leave the general subject of card table artifice without giving some consideration to the ancient and honorable game whose title furnishes the headline for this paragraph. Only three cards are used, but the more players the merrier. The banker, or dealer, shows the faces of any three cards, generally using one Ace, and deals or throws them face down in a row on the table. Now he lays even money or perhaps two to one, that no player can pick out the Ace. In appearance it is the simplest and easiest proposition a better could desire. In reality it is pure chance or accident if he calls the turn. The cards are thrown so slowly, and apparently so openly, that it seems like robbing the dealer to cover his odds.

This is really one of the most subtle and ingenious gambling games ever devised to win money honestly with cards. We use the word "honestly" in the sense that it may be applied to qualify any procedure in a game of chance, which gives the player a known percentage for or against him. In this instance it is two to one in favor of the dealer; but as the dealer lays the odds of two to one, and the player keeps his eyes open, it would indicate that the player has the better chance of winning. The dealer lays out the three cards, and the player takes his choice. One of them is the Ace, and there is no hocus-pocus after the deal. Should the player select the Ace he wins the money. But the player's chances are lessened just because he watches the deal. Were he to make the selection at hap-hazard, his chances of one to two, against the dealer's odds of two to one, would make it an even break. The banker's advantage lies in his ability to make the deal or throw. The cards are usually crimped lengthwise, the faces being concave, so the dealer may pick them up easily by the ends. There is no other advantage in the crimp, and the game is sometimes dealt with straight cards. When being crimped the cards are placed together, so that all will be bent alike. The deal or "throw" is performed as follows:

Lay the three crimped cards in a row on the table face down. Pick up one of the indifferent cards, by the ends, near the right side corners, with the right-hand thumb and second finger, and show the face of this card to the players. Now place this card fairly over the Ace, letting the left sides of the two cards touch, and pick up the Ace with the thumb and the third finger. Now the right hand holds the two cards, their left side edges touching, and about half an inch of space between the opposite sides; the top card being held by the second finger and thumb, and the bottom card, or Ace, by the third finger and thumb. Show the Ace to the company, keep the right hand suspended about six inches from the table, pick up the third card with the left hand, and show it to the company. (See Fig. 62.) Now turn the faces down, move the right hand over towards the left and with a slight downward swing release the upper card, letting it drop flatly on the left side of the table by quickly withdrawing the right hand to its former position; the rapid withdrawal getting the lower card out of the way. As the right second finger releases the top card it instantly seizes the lower card and the third finger is straightened out, so when the right hand is again stationary at its first position over the table, the players may see that the finger that held the upper card is still doing duty, and the finger which held the lower card is now idle. Now move the left hand over towards the right, and drop its card there, then again move the right hand over and drop the last card between the other two.

As described above, the blind takes place in the first movement or throw. The right hand apparently drops the bottom card first, but in reality the top is thrown. The action is neither hurried or slow, and especially, not jerky. There is no hesitation after the faces are turned down, and the movements of both hands are made uniformly and gracefully while the three cards are being laid out.

There is very little difficulty in acquiring the ability to throw the top

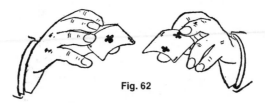

Fig. 62

card first, or in changing the positions of the second and third fingers as the top card falls, and a little practice at the game enables an amateur to afford endless amusement or entertainment to his friends with this cunning play. The proper way to introduce it is to make the throw several times in the natural order, that is, by dropping the under card first, while explaining the game to the company. The Ace should be picked up by either hand in the order it happens to fall, and be held at either the top or bottom position in the right hand, and the faces shown before each throw. Then the blind throw is made and the guessing and fun begins. When the deal is performed by a finished artist, it is absolutely impossible for the keenest eye to detect the ruse. Even when the process, or nature of the blind is understood, the player has no greater advantage save that he knows enough not to bet. The particular card cannot be followed with the eye, and if the knowing player were to bet on a blind throw once, the dealer can make his next throw regular. The dealer himself is as hopelessly lost, if guessing against another who can throw equally as well.

A second method of making the throw or deal is to hold the two right-hand cards between the second finger and thumb only, the right third finger taking no part in the action and being held rather ostentatiously straight out. When the top card is thrown, the left little finger is moved in under the end of the third finger, and the tip catches and holds the corner of the lower card, while the second finger releases both, so as to let the top card fall. Then the second finger instantly retakes its original position, and the little finger is released. The action of the little finger is completely covered by the position of the third finger. This method is perhaps more subtle, as it appears quite impossible to throw the top card without dropping both.

An addition to the game is made by putting in a crimp or upturn in a corner of the Ace. Then several throws are made, and a player finds he can locate the Ace "just for fun" every time. When perfect confidence is inspired, and the cupidity of the player tempts him to cover the odds, a throw is made, the player selects the card with the corner turned, and is amazed to find he has missed the "cinch." In a confidence game, the corner of the Ace is turned by a "capper," who seizes an opportunity when the careless (?) dealer turns to expectorate, or on any pretext neglects his game for a moment. But the crimp can be put in, taken out, and again put in the corner of another card during the procedure of the throw.

To crimp the corner, pick up the Ace with the second finger and thumb of right hand, second finger at middle of end, and let the third fingertip rest on top of the card close to second finger. Then catch the corner with the little finger and squeeze it in, pressing down with third fingertip, and the corner is crimped upward. The corner is turned down again by slipping the third fingertip over the end, and pulling up; and pressing down on the corner with the little fingertip. Either action can be performed in an instant as the card is picked up. Now to make the "corner" throw the Ace is picked up, shown, and crimped, then the second card is picked up with the third finger and thumb and shown, the left hand picks up and shows the third card, and a natural throw is made which leaves the Ace in the middle. Then the right hand picks up the right-hand card, shows it, crimps the corner, picks up the Ace, shows it, and the left hand picks up the last card. Now the right hand holds the two turned corner cards, but the fact that the upper one is crimped cannot be seen because of the positions of the fingers, even when the face of the under one, which is the Ace, is shown. This time a blind throw is made, the right hand dropping the top card first with its corner turned, then the left-hand card is thrown, and long ere this the right hand has turned down the corner of the Ace and it is dropped innocently in the middle.

The process of turning and reversing the corners requires as much skill and cleverness as making the throw. All details of the game should be perfected before it is attempted in company, and nothing but careful practice before a mirror will enable an amateur to perform the action in anything like a satisfactory manner. But there is not a single card feat in the whole calendar that will give as good returns for the amount of practice required, or that will mystify as greatly, or cause as much amusement, or bear so much repetition, as this little game; and for these reasons we believe it worthy of unstinted effort to master thoroughly.

Mexican Three Card Monte. — When the game is played in the following manner the better has no possible chance to win, and yet it appears simpler and easier than the other. An entirely different subterfuge is employed by the dealer. The three cards are left perfectly flat. Sometimes the four corners are turned the very least upwards, merely enough to allow one card to be slipped under the other when lying face down on the table, but the bend is not necessary.

The dealer now shows the faces of the three cards, and slowly lays them in a row. Then he makes a pretense of confusing the company by changing their places on the table. Now in explaining the game, he shows the faces of the cards by picking up one, and with it turning over the others, by slipping it under them and tilting them over face up. Then he turns them down again in the same manner and lays down the third card. This procedure is continued until the company understands the game, and the manner of showing the cards has grown customary, as it were.

When the bet is made and the player indicates his choice the dealer at once proclaims that the player has lost, and to prove it he picks one of the other cards and with it rapidly turns over the player's card, and then the third card, and the third card proves to be the Ace.

Of course the better can really select the Ace every time, but he is not permitted to turn the cards himself, or touch them at all. The dealer exchanges the card he picks up for the player's card, and again exchanges that for the third card, when apparently turning them over. The exchange is absolutely impossible to note, and is made as follows:

Hold the card in the right hand between the tips of thumb and first

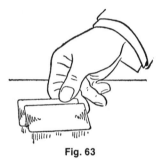

Fig. 63

finger close to right inner end corner, thumb on top. Slide the free side of this card under the right side of the card on the table, until it is about two-thirds concealed, but half an inch exposed at the outer end. (See Fig. 63.) This will bring the upper, inner end corner of the table card against the tip of the second finger. Now shift the thumb to the corner of the table card, holding it against the second finger, carrying it to the left and turning over the lower card with the tip of the first finger. (See Fig. 64.)

Of course there is no hesitation in the action. The slipping of the hand card under the table card, and the turning over of the hand card, is done with one movement. The table card is not shown at this stage, but is slipped under the third card and the exchange is again made in like manner. Then the last card is shown.

This method of exchanging can be worked with the first method of dealing or throwing, but in such case the cards are not crimped.

To perform this feat perfectly a cloth covered table must be used. When the table is of polished wood the cards slip about, and it is much more difficult to slip the hand card into position under the other.

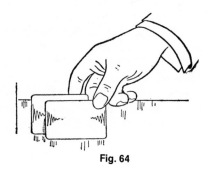

Fig. 64

LEGERDEMAIN

There is no branch of conjuring that so fully repays the amateur for his labor and study as slight-of-hand with cards. The artist is always sure of a comprehensive and appreciative audience. There is no amusement or pastime in the civilized world so prevalent as card games, and almost everybody loves a good trick. But the special advantage in this respect is that the really clever card-handler can dispense with the endless devices and preparations that encumber the performer in other branches. He is ever prepared for the most unexpected demands upon his ability to amuse or mystify, and he can sustain his reputation with nothing but the family deck and his nimble fingers, making his exhibition all the more startling because of its known impromptu nature and simple accessories.

To the student who wishes to make the most rapid progress toward the actual performance of tricks, we suggest that he first take up the study and practice of our "System of Blind Shuffles" as taught in the first part of this book, acquiring thorough proficiency in forming and using the "jog" and "break," which make this style of shuffle possible. We are aware that all conjurers advise the shift or pass, as the first accomplishment, and while we do not belittle the merits of the shift when perfectly performed, we insist that all or any of the various methods of executing it, are among the most difficult feats the student will be called upon to acquire, and imposing such a task at the outset has a most discouraging effect. But so far as we can learn from the exhibitions and literature of conjurers, not one of them knows of, or at least employs or writes of, a satisfactory substitute; hence their entire dependence upon that artifice to produce certain results.

When the blind shuffles with the coincident jog and break are thoroughly understood, the student should take up our "System of Palming," also treated in the first part, paying particular attention to the "bottom palm," and with even a moderate degree of skill in these accomplishments he will be enabled to perform many of the best tricks that conjurers make entirely dependent on the shift.

For example, the common process for obtaining possession of a selected card when it is replaced in the deck, is to insert the little finger over it, make a shift bringing the lower packet with the selected card to the top, palm it off in the right hand, and give the deck to the spectator to shuffle. Now it may be a matter of opinion, but we think it would appear quite as natural if the performer were to shuffle the deck himself, immediately when the card is replaced in the middle, then palm off and hand the deck to the spectator to shuffle. If the spectator shuffles for the purpose of concealing any knowledge of its whereabouts, the performer's shuffle may reasonably be expected to increase the impression that it is hopelessly lost, and especially because his shuffle is made without the least hesitation, turn, swing, concealment or patter, and apparently in the most natural and regular way. Then the performer's shuffle gives a tacit reason for holding the deck while the card is inserted, instead of permitting the spectator to take the deck in his own hands. Well executed, the blind shuffle brings the card to the top or bottom at will, defying the closest scrutiny to detect the manipulation. The card is then palmed while squaring up, and the deck now handed over for further shuffling.

Should the performer wish to palm off the selected card without employing a shuffle, we believe the "Diagonal Palm-Shift" is easier and far more imperceptible than the shifting of the two packets and then palming, assuming that the different processes are performed equally well. For this reason we suggest the early acquirement of the mentioned shift.

However, the enthusiast will not rest until every sleight in the calendar has been perfectly mastered, so that he may be enabled to nonplus and squelch that particularly obnoxious but ever present individual, who with his smattering of the commoner slights always knows "exactly how it is done." Acquiring the art is in itself a most fascinating pastime, and the student will need no further incentive the moment the least progress is made.

The finished card-table expert will experience little or no difficulty in accomplishing the various sleights that lie at the bottom of the conjurer's tricks. The principal feats have been already mastered in acquiring the blind shuffles, blind cuts, bottom deal, second deal, palming and replacing, the run, the crimp, culling, and stocking; and his trained fingers will readily accommodate themselves to any new positions or actions. But the mere ability to execute the slights by no means fits him for the stage or even a drawing-room entertainment. In this phase of card-handling, as with card-table artifice, we are of the opinion that the less the company knows about the dexterity of the performer, the better it answers his purpose. A much greater interest is taken in the tricks, and the denouement of each causes infinitely more amazement, when the entire procedure has been conducted in an ordinary manner, and quite free of ostensible cleverness at prestidigitation. If the performer cannot resist the temptation to parade his digital ability, it will mar the effect of his endeavors much less by adjuring the exhibition of such sleights as palming and producing, single-hand shifts, changes, etc., until the wind up of the entertainment. But the sleights should be employed only as a means to an end.

The amateur conjurer who is not naturally blessed with a "gift of the gab" should rehearse his "patter" or monologue as carefully as his action. The simplest trick should be appropriately clothed with chicanery or plausible sophistry which apparently explains the procedure, but in reality describes about the contrary of what takes place.

The principal slights employed in card tricks, that are not touched upon in the first part of this book, are known as "forcing," "changes," "transformations," and various methods of locating and producing selected cards. We shall also describe other methods of shifting and palming. We should mention that a shift is termed by the conjurer a "pass."

SHIFTS

Single-Handed Shift. — This is known to conjurers as the "Charlier Pass," and we presume was invented by the famous magician of that name.

Hold the deck in the left hand face down, between the thumb tip at one side and first joints of second and third fingers at opposite side, first joint of little finger at end, and first finger extended at bottom. To make the shift release the lower portion of the deck with the thumb, letting it fall into the palm (see Fig. 65), then push up the finger side of the fallen portion, with the first fingertip, until it reaches the thumb which is still

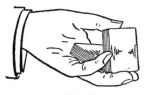

Fig. 65

supporting the upper portion. Now extend the second and third fingers slightly so that the thumb side of the upper portion will pass the upturned side of the lower portion (see Fig. 66), then straighten out the first finger allowing the upper portion to drop down into the palm and the lower portion on top of it.

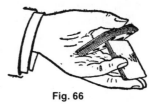

Fig. 66

The little finger held at the middle of the end is of great assistance in this shift, giving better control of both portions, and enabling the performer to hold the deck much nearer a vertical position. The shift is invariably made with a slight swing, or up-and-down motion of the hand. It can be executed very rapidly, and is the favorite one-handed shift with most experts. It is usually employed to receive and bring a selected card to the top. As the performer extends the deck to have the selected card returned, he raises the upper portion with the tip of the thumb, and the selected card is naturally placed in the opening. In this position the shift is half made, the condition being the same as when the first movement of dropping the lower portion into the palm takes place. The performer now with an up or down motion, or swing toward the person, tilts up the lower portion with the first finger and the shift is made, bringing the selected card to the top to be disposed of as desired.

The Longitudinal Shift. — This shift, for which we have to thank no one, is given a very long name, but the reader who is interested sufficiently to practice the process, will find it a very short shift and comparatively an easy one.

Hold the deck in the left hand, face down, first joint of thumb at middle of one side, first joint of second finger, and second joint of third finger, at opposite side, and the lower corner of the deck fitting in between the third and little fingers, at the base of little finger, the first finger curled up against the bottom. Now bring the right hand over; second, third and little fingers at outer end, first finger curled up on top, thumb at inner end. Separate the deck with the right thumb, at the inner end only, about half an inch, and press the third joint of the little finger in between the corners of the two packets to be shuffled. (See Fig. 67.) Now the deck is ready for the shift, but the right hand may be withdrawn without disclosing the break at the inner corner, or the fact that the little finger runs between the packets. The left thumb and finger hold the packets firmly together and the deck could not have a more innocent appearance.

To make the shift, bring the right thumb against the side of the first finger, straighten out the first finger, press the end of the lower packet in against the left little finger and down against the curled-up first finger, with the four right-hand fingers; and with the left little finger and thumb

Fig. 67

draw off the upper packet toward the person (see Fig. 68), and as the lower packet springs into the right palm bring the upper packet back underneath.

The right thumb takes no part in the shift, and a favorable feature of the operation is that it may be performed without the right hand appearing to be used at all. The right fingers may be held almost straight, and the palm well away from the deck, the hand being slightly closed as the lower packet springs up. It can be made with practically no noise, and the action is well covered.

If desired this shift can be made with almost the whole deck exposed, by employing right second and third fingers only at end, and keeping first finger curled up on top. In this case the right thumb tip catches the end of the lower packet as it springs up.

The Open Shift. — This is another outcome of our constant but ever failing efforts to devise a perfect shift, and incidentally one that is not readily anticipated by the manner of holding the deck. The particular feature of this method is the open position in which the cards are held, the entire deck being exposed to view.

Hold the deck in the left hand, the first joint of the thumb at one side,

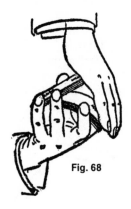

Fig. 68

first joints of second, third, and little fingers at opposite side, the little finger holding a break between the two packets near the corner, and the little and third fingers being separated about one inch. The first finger is curled up against the bottom. Bring the right hand over, and seize the ends of deck close to right side corners, with the second finger and thumb tips, the thumb seizing only the lower packet below the break, the first finger curled up on top. (See Fig. 69.) The left third and little fingers take no part in the action and are held idly out of the way.

To make the shift, curl the right first finger back over the side of the

Fig. 69

deck, between the left little and third fingers, until the root of the finger-nail rests against the edge of the top card. Now press the upper packet against the left thumb and downward by straightening out the right first finger, at the same time drawing the lower packet to the right and upward with the right thumb and second finger (see Fig. 70), and as the sides clear each other tilt the left side of the lower or right-hand packet up on top. The upper packet should not fall into the left hand. It must be caught by the curled-up first finger and first joints of the other left fingers, as it clears the side of the under packet. The left thumb never leaves its position against the side of the upper packet, and the tip should be held sufficiently above it to receive the lower packet as it is brought on top. The left little finger is not inserted between the two packets, but merely holds the break.

The shift can be made like a flash, and with the cards in perfect order. When executed perfectly, the only sound is the slipping of one packet over the other. There is no snap or crack, and it is in every way worthy of the practice necessary to acquire it. With the face of the deck turned upward it produces a "transformation" that ranks with the best of them.

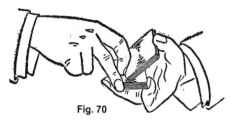

Fig. 70

The same shift may be made with the deck held flat in the palm, the left thumb lying idly across the top, and the first finger at the side with the others, but we much prefer the former position though it is a great deal more difficult. The latter position is an excellent one when it is necessary to make a shift that is apparently a simple cut, in which event the right hand does not tilt its packet on top. The hands immediately separate and the under packet is placed on top when desired.

The S. W. E. Shift. — We have not dubbed the following process with our initials because we wish to appear "big on the bills," but merely to give it a name. Still, we must confess to some satisfaction in having originated what we believe to be the most rapid, and, for certain pur-poses, the most perfect shift ever devised. The method is practically the same as the "Longitudinal," but as the deck is held crosswise it is much more rapid. The position is open and natural, and the shift possesses many advantages for conjuring purposes.

Hold the deck in the left hand, face down, first joint of the thumb against middle of one end, second, third and little fingers against the opposite or lower end, little finger holding a break between the two packets at end, by the corner of the lower packet being between the little and third fingers, the little finger lying partially across the corner of the

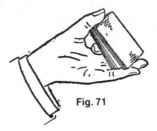

Fig. 71

under packet. (See Fig. 71.) This position, like that of the "Longitudinal," allows the tips of the second, third and little fingers to appear over the top of the deck, and the fact that there is a break is not apparent to a spectator. The first finger is curled up against the bottom. The break is held only at the lower end, and at the inside, the other fingers and thumb holding the packet firmly together.

Now bring the right hand over the lower or right-hand end of the deck, and seize the sides as close as possible to the lower corners, between the second and third fingertips and thumb, the first finger curled up on top out of the way. This leaves at least two-thirds of the deck in view. (See Fig. 72.) To make the shift raise the right thumb to the edge of the side, draw the top packet in and down with the left thumb and little finger, and press the lower packet out and down, between the right second and

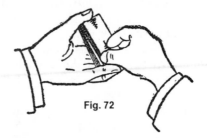

Fig. 72

third fingertips and the left first finger which is curled up underneath; the left second finger at the end helps to control the lower packet as it is pressed out. This action will tilt the opposite sides of both packets upward, and as they clear each other the right thumb tip catches the under packet, and the left third finger catches the upper packet and it is brought back underneath. (See Fig. 73.)

When the shift is mastered the entire action is accomplished by a pressure in opposite directions on the lower packet, and the packets reverse like a flash, but of course it must be practiced slowly until the knack is obtained. The positions of the hands may be taken with easy deliberation, as there is no indication that a shift is meditated. It may be made with the hands stationary without exposing the action. With the deck face up it makes an instantaneous "transformation," and the position of the deck permits the operator to get a glimpse of the index without being observed.

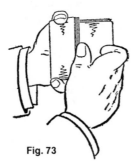

Fig. 73

The shift may be made with the right hand almost entirely covering the deck, but this alters the whole character and aim of the process, the main endeavor is to make it as open and free from concealment as possible.

The Diagonal Palm-Shift. — The plan of having one or several selected cards inserted in the deck, then forcing them through slightly diagonally, and twisting them out to the top or bottom, is well known to most conjurers, and by some is treated as a blind shuffle. That the process is not satisfactory is seen by the fact that it is seldom or never employed, and but rarely even mentioned in any list of card sleights. Our efforts to improve, or rather to combine the first part of this manœuvre with a process for palming the inserted cards, instead of placing them on top or bottom of the deck, is shown in the following description. The action is silent, rapid, undetectable if well performed, and takes place under the ordinary movement of passing the deck to be shuffled.

Hold the deck in the left hand, by sides, between the first joints of thumb, and second, third and little fingers, first finger curled up at bottom. Allow spectator to insert selected card in outer end of deck, pushing it in until about half an inch only protrudes. Now bring the right hand over deck with the little finger at side corner of protruding card, second and third fingers at middle of end, and first finger close to end corner, and the thumb close to the inner end corner of the deck. Apparently push the card straight home, but really push the protruding

Fig. 74

end with the right little finger, about a quarter of an inch to the left, so that the right first finger can push the tilted corner down the side of the deck, the card moving slightly diagonally, and the opposite corner just grazing the right thumb, and protruding about three-quarters of an inch. The left third and little fingers are released sufficiently to allow the card to protrude at the side. The left thumb now takes the place of the right first finger, pushing the corner flush with side of deck. (See Fig. 74.)

The diagonal position of the selected card is now perfectly concealed, and the deck is held in a natural and regular manner. A little practice at the diagonal slide enables one to get the card in that position instantaneously. The next action is to palm the selected card in the left hand, as the right passes the deck to be shuffled.

With the left little finger against the side of card, swing or turn it inward, using the right thumb as a pivot, straighten out left first, second, and third fingers, catching the outer end as it turns, and at the same time sliding pack outward and to the right, the left hand turning over and inward with the palmed card (see Fig. 75) and the little finger slipped to the end.

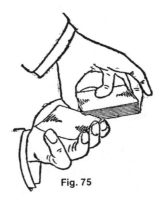

Fig. 75

There should be no force or twist employed, the card running out as freely as though drawn. The card and the deck must continue on the same plane until quite free of each other. The left little finger may press the side of the card very slightly upward, so that as it is palmed it will bend into instead of away from the left hand. As the card is being turned by the little finger the left thumb is raised, letting the right thumb with the corner of deck pass under it, so that the card can lie parallel with, but still above, the left palm. As the deck is slid out, the right thumb slides along the side of the card, and it is not actually palmed until the hands are almost free of each other.

The whole action may be made quick as a flash and without a sound,

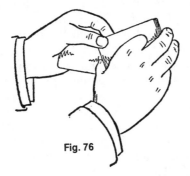

Fig. 76

yet when performed quite slowly is still a perfect blind. The left hand may seize the deck by the corner, between the first finger and thumb, as the card is palmed, leaving the right hand free (see Fig. 76); but the beauty of the shift is in the natural and simple manner of palming the selected card, by the ordinary movement the right hand makes in passing the deck to be shuffled.

We wish to particularly impress our readers with the merits of this palm-shift. It is not difficult if a proper understanding of the action is obtained, and it is of very great assistance in card tricks. It dispenses to a great extent with the regular shifts and blind shuffles, and it can be accomplished under the very nose of a shrewd spectator without an inkling of what is taking place. The usual procedure of card-handlers is to insert the little finger over the selected card, shift the two packets and palm the card from the top in the right hand. This process takes more time, the shift must be concealed by a partial turn, swing or drop of the hands; and to palm, the deck must be covered at least for an instant. In the palm-shift described the card is placed in its diagonal position with apparently the customary movement of squaring up, and the rest is accomplished, as it were, by handing the deck to be shuffled.

Several cards may be palmed together, when inserted at different points, or from one point, or from top, or bottom. If the top card is to be shifted, it is slipped into the same diagonal position and held in place by the right little finger being curled up on top. The action is the same. When the single-card palm-shift is acquired, the rest will come easily.

THE BLIND SHUFFLE FOR SECURING SELECTED CARD

Hold the deck across the left hand and when selected card is inserted, form break over it with left little finger close to side corner. Now seize the deck by the ends from above with the right thumb and second finger, and close to right side corners; the right thumb taking up the break at the end; and with the left thumb and fingers turn the deck down on its side into the left palm in the position given for blind shuffling, the right hand remaining stationary, the thumb and finger being the pivots, as it were, allowing the deck to turn, and the right thumb still holding the break. The action appears quite natural, and enables the thumb to hold the break without moving. Immediately begin the shuffle. Under-cut to about half portion above break, shuffle off to break, in-jog first card and shuffle off. Then under-cut to in-jog and shuffle off. This action leaves the selected card at the bottom. Square up, palm bottom card in left hand and pass deck to spectator to shuffle.

In making the bottom palm it matters little whether one or several cards are palmed, and the action is quicker if not particular about the number.

Of course the selected card may be brought to the top just as easily, as an understanding of the "System of Blind Shuffles" makes clear. The only difference in the foregoing action would be to jog the second card instead of the first when the break is reached, and then under-cut to the jog and throw on top, instead of shuffling off. But we consider the left-hand work, or bottom palming, far superior to palming from the top, and the several methods given in the first part of the book will be found instantaneous, undetectable, and up to the present unknown and consequently not suspected.

FORCING

Many of the best card tricks are dependent upon having the company select one or more certain or particular cards, which after being replaced in the deck and shuffled, are reproduced in various ways at some stage of the proceeding. Compelling the company to select such particular cards, without in the least suspecting the choice is influenced in any manner, is called "forcing." It is probably used to a greater extent than any other expedient, excepting the shift.

The usual method of "forcing" is to bring the particular card to the middle of the deck by means of a shift, and hold its location by inserting the little finger at that point. Now the performer, advancing the hands toward the spectator, opens the deck slightly fanwise, pushing the cards with the left thumb one under the other into the right palm, the right fingers aiding the operation; apparently to enable the spectator to take any card he may wish. As he shows an indication of selecting one, the passing movement, which by this time has reached the located card, is stopped and the located card exposed a trifle more than the others. An unsuspicious person will naturally select the one easiest to seize. In any case, he can get no other, as the fingers and thumbs of the performer's hands hold the balance of the cards firmly. Should the spectator's fingers touch other than the particular card the performer carelessly draws back and closes the deck as though he thought a card were seized, then, with an excuse, opens the deck again. But a little practice at forcing enables a clever performer to almost place the particular card in the spectator's hand without the least show of design. The action should be easy, but rather rapid, and if the first spectator approached shows a disposition to be over discriminating he should be passed immediately and the next one may display greater alacrity. But should the first individual get the wrong card, there is no harm done. The performer passes on to a more obliging spectator and forces the particular card, and completes the trick in contemplation. Then the first card drawn is returned to the deck and used in some trick that does not require a prior knowledge. If two or three cards are noted and located together the force becomes simpler, as a greater liberty may be allowed in the selection and, of course, the order of the several cards enables the performer to determine the particular card as it is selected.

PALMING

In addition to the methods given in the first part of our book, which we consider the best for general purposes, we shall describe several processes that may be employed advantageously under special circumstances.

The top cards may be palmed apparently without touching the deck in the following manner: Hold the deck across the left palm, the little finger well inserted under the cards to be palmed, the first, second and third fingers holding the cards firmly in place. Now move the right hand, through some natural motive, over the left, and as it passes within one inch or two straighten out the left-hand fingers, forcing the cards up into the right palm with the little finger, which is under them. The right hand either continues its movement as it slightly closes over the palmed cards or else seizes the deck in a manner to expose it fully, and the left hand makes some gesture or natural movement.

A simple way to palm one top card is to push it slightly over the side under cover of the right hand, then press down on its outer-end corner with the right little fingertip, and it will spring up into the right palm.

In all cases of palming the deck should be covered for the smallest possible space of time, and the covering and exposing should be made

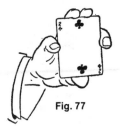

Fig. 77

under some natural pretext, such as squaring up the cards, or passing the deck to the other hand, or changing its position in the hand, or turning it over.

The Back Palm. — We are afraid the above title is a misnomer. The cards to be concealed are transferred to the back of the hand. Hold the card in the right hand face up between the tip of the thumb at one end and tips of second and third fingers at opposite end, the first joints of the

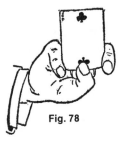

Fig. 78

first and little fingers hold the sides. (See Fig. 77.) To make the "palm," slip the tips of the second and third fingers under the end of the card and curl them down until they come under the thumb, at the same time pushing the card outward with the thumb until the inner corners reach the first and little fingers, which hold it in position. (See Fig. 78.) Now, straighten out the four fingers, clipping the corners of the card between the little and third fingertips and the first and second fingertips, and the card lies along the back of the hand. (See Fig. 79.)

To bring it to the front again curl the four fingers again into the palm, straighten the first fingertip a little so that the thumb may take its place holding the card, then draw the card as far as possible toward the wrist

Fig. 79

with the thumb and little finger, straightening out the other fingers, then clip the corner between the first and second fingertips, and slide the little finger along the side of the card until it is straight out, this time clipping the outer corners between the same fingers instead of palming in the usual way.

Several cards may be transferred back and forth in this manner, and one at a time may be produced from the back without showing the rest. Perfection in the feat enables a performer to show both sides of the hand, transferring the cards as it is turned over. A slight up-and-down motion and a backward turn of the wrist is used.

As an exhibition of dexterity this is probably unsurpassed in card manipulation, but it is of little aid in the performance of tricks. However, everything may be put to some use, and the back palm once helped us out of a difficult situation — "but that is another story."

CHANGES

Under this general heading we shall describe several of the best methods known for secretly exchanging one or several cards separated from the pack, for others in the pack or held in the other hand.

The Top Change. — Hold the deck in the left hand crosswise, face

Fig. 80

down, the thumb resting across the top. Hold the card to be exchanged in the right hand between the thumb and first fingertips, thumb on top, finger under. Now the hands are brought together for an instant by an easy swing, both hands moving in the same general direction but one hand faster than the other. As they meet the left thumb pushes the top card slightly over the side, the right hand places its card on top and clips the protruding card between the tips of the first and second fingers, carrying it off (see Fig. 80), the left thumb retaining the now top card and sliding it back into position on the deck. In theory it seems that this action will be very easily noticed. In practice, if cleverly performed, it is almost impossible to detect. The general movement or swing of the hands is not stopped when the exchange is made but continued until they are separated again by some little distance, and the swing should be taken naturally, with some ulterior motive, such as placing the card on the table or giving it to some one to hold. A slight turn of the person may bring the hands easily together. The swing may be made in any direction, in or out, up or down, to the right or left, the one hand following or passing the other, but in no case stopping until well separated again.

The Bottom Change. — In this process the action is much the same, the difference being that the card in the right hand is passed to the bottom of the deck, the right hand carrying off the top card as before.

Fig. 81

Hold the right-hand card between the thumb and first and second fingertips, first finger on top. Hold the deck with the thumb and first finger, dropping the other fingers slightly to receive the right-hand card, drawing it back under the deck as the hands separate. The top card is pushed over as before and carried off by the right thumb and first finger. (See Fig. 81.) The swing of the hands is made in the same manner. The only difficulty in this change is getting the card fairly back under the deck with the left fingers.

The Palm Change. — In this process an entirely different subterfuge is employed, and it is probably the most ingenious ever devised for the purpose.

The two cards to be exchanged are held in the right hand by the ends between the second and third fingertips and the thumb, and close together, so that when shown to the company they appear as one. The right hand is now turned palm down and the left hand apparently takes the card that was exposed, laying it on the table, but in reality takes the second card, leaving the other one palmed in the right hand. This is done by seizing both cards between the left thumb and second and third fingers, and drawing out the upper one with the thumb and pressing the lower one up into the right palm with the left fingers as the top one is drawn off. (See Fig. 82.)

This change is one of the simplest and easiest feats in the whole range

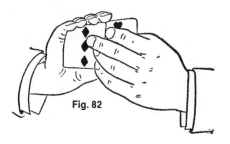

Fig. 82

of card sleights, and yet one of the most useful and undetectable. The action should be performed in about the same time and manner that would ordinarily be taken in transferring a card from one hand to the other.

The Double-Palm Change. — This method may be employed to exchange one or several cards. The cards to be exchanged lie in a packet on the table face up. The other cards are secretly palmed face down in the left hand. The left hand now picks up the packet on the table by the sides, between the thumb and second and third fingertips, and transfers the packet to the right hand. As the left hand turns palm up the right hand palms the packet just picked up and seizes the packet in the left

Fig. 83

palm by the sides, carrying it slowly and openly away, and the left hand is seen empty. (See Fig. 83.)

As the right hand palms the upper cards the left first finger curls up under the palmed cards, bending them upward, thus enabling the right hand to seize them easier and also effectually taking out the crimp or bend that may have been caused while so closely palmed.

The only objectionable feature of this change is that the right hand carries the packet away by the sides, while it may have been noticed that the packet first in view was seized by the ends. But this is a splendid change for many purposes.

TRANSFORMATIONS. TWO HANDS

The card conjurer in many instances purposely produces the wrong card, and when his error (?) is proclaimed by the company or the individual, he coolly proposes to "make good" by transforming the wrong card into the right one. This is usually done by placing the wrong card on the top or bottom of the deck and making the "transformation" with the aid of both hands or only one.

First Method. — The right hand holds the wrong card, which has just been exhibited; the left hand holds the deck between the thumb and second, third and little fingers at the sides, first finger at end, the back of deck to the palm and the selected card on the bottom. The deck is inverted or the hand turned palm down, so that the bottom card cannot be seen. The right hand now openly places the wrong card on the bottom of the deck and carelessly shows the palm empty. Then the tips of the right-hand fingers are placed against the bottom of the deck, both hands turning it up in view, showing the wrong card that was just placed there. But as the deck is turned up the right fingertips push the wrong card up against the left first finger, about one inch, so that the right palm a little below the base of the fingers may be pressed against the selected card, which is the next one. This card is drawn down slowly by pressing against it, the downward movement being apparently to give the company a full view of the wrong card. (See Fig. 84.) When the ends of the two cards pass each other the lower card is tilted on top and the right palm again covers the whole deck, carrying the selected card along, and the left first finger presses the wrong card back into position. The

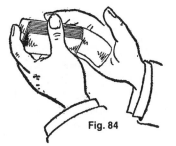

Fig. 84

performer now pronounces the talismanic word, shows the right hand empty, and the transformation accomplished.

Cleverly executed, this is a very effective sleight, and there is little or no difficulty in acquiring it. It may be performed rapidly or slowly, as the operator fancies.

Second Method. — Hold the deck in the left hand, between the thumb and second, third and little fingers, at sides, first fingertip against the back near end, and the back, or top card, the selected card; the wrong card being on the bottom, or placed there and held in full view. To make the transformation bring the right hand over the deck with the four fingertips against the end. Slide or push the selected card with the first fingertip up against the right-hand finger ends, drawing the deck down toward the wrist until it clears the lower end of the selected card, which is pressed into the right palm by the left first finger. (See Fig. 85.) Then slide the deck back to its first position. This sleight may be made in an instant and the action is fully covered.

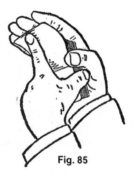

Fig. 85

Third Method. — Hold the deck in left hand, resting on its side across the third joints of the four fingers, tip of thumb on top side, face to the company. Cover face with the right hand held quite flatly; tilt top side of deck slightly toward right hand; drop left thumb to the back, and push up the top card. As it comes above the side bring the right hand up and back over the left thumb, catching the up-coming card against the side of the hand and palming it as it is carried over, the left thumb aiding the palming by pressing the card home. The left thumb then instantly retakes its position on the top side of the deck. The movement of the right hand is made apparently to show the bottom card. The right hand now again covers the deck for an instant, leaving the palmed card there.

Palming the back card in this manner may be done very rapidly, but a slow movement is satisfactory.

Fourth Method. — The action of this transformation is identical with the Third Method, but the first and little fingers are held against the ends of the deck close to the lower corners, the thumb and second and third fingers at the top and bottom sides as before. In this position the

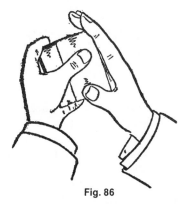

Fig. 86

deck is held much more firmly, and it becomes easier for the left thumb to push up one card at a time, the fingers at the ends restraining the other cards. The right hand performs its part as in the Third Method. The improvement is our own. (See Fig. 86.)

Fifth Method. — Hold the deck in the left hand, thumb and three fingers at opposite sides, first finger against end. Cover the deck with the right hand but run the right thumb underneath. Now draw out the under card with the right thumb, palming it, and again cover the deck, leaving the palmed card on top.

Sixth Method. — Now we introduce another "homemade" article, and consequently unknown up to the present. We think it is very pretty.

Hold the deck in the left hand by the ends, between the tips of the thumb and second and third fingers, the first finger resting against the side and the little fingertip against the bottom, close to the corner, the face of the deck to the company and the finger end down. Bring the right hand forward so that the little fingertips meet at the corner of deck, the palm partly facing the company and showing the hand empty, the wrists being about six inches apart. Now, with the left little fingertip push the corner of the lower card slightly over the side, and clip it with the right little fingertip, so that it is firmly held between the two tips (see Fig. 87), and press it down against the left third finger, turning the right

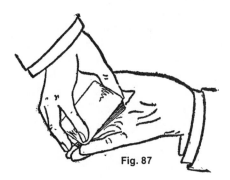

Fig. 87

hand over and moving the upper end of the deck to the left at the same time. This action will cause the lower card to swing out at the upper end, and it is caught and palmed by the right hand as the hand turns over. The left little finger is extended as the turn is made, pressing the card firmly against the right fingers. (See Fig. 88.) Now the right hand immediately seizes the deck close to the lower end, and the left hand releasing it, is shown empty. Then the left hand again seizes the deck, but this time by the sides, with the little finger against the lower end. The right hand is now released and passed rapidly downward over the deck, leaving the palmed card on top, and the right hand is shown empty. The left little finger at the end aids the replacing by catching the palmed card as the right hand is drawn down.

Of course, the performer makes the movements of passing the deck

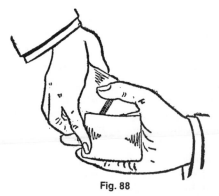

Fig. 88

from hand to hand and showing the hands empty, ostensibly to prove that no palming takes place. The act of palming, if cleverly performed, is absolutely undetectable; the right hand turning over just in time and sufficiently to cover the card coming out, but not obstructing the continued view of the face of the deck. The actual palm can be made as rapidly as desired and without a sound. Our readers should cultivate this "transformation," though it may take some little practice to acquire perfectly.

TRANSFORMATIONS. ONE HAND

First Method. — Hold the deck in the left hand, the thumb well extended across the face, first finger at end, second and little fingers at side and third finger curled in as far as possible underneath. Grip the top card with the thumb and draw it back, tilting up the deck with the third finger until the top card clears the side (see Fig. 89), then press the top card down between the curled-up finger and deck by bringing the thumb again

Fig. 89

to its original position across top. (See Fig. 90.) The third and little finger ends steady the pack as it is tilted upward, but the first finger takes no part in the action. The top card must be gripped well into the root of the thumb and drawn back as far as possible as the deck is being tilted up.

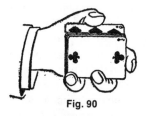

Fig. 90

The action should be covered by a swing, and as it is extremely difficult to execute without some noise the company might be informed that if they cannot see the "transformation" they will be permitted to hear it. The rapidity of the action is proportionate to the skill of the performer, and it may be made with the hand in any position.

Second Method. — The following process is another of our innovations, and it will be found easy, extremely rapid and without the least noise, a rare combination in one-handed manœuvers.

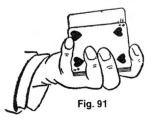

Fig. 91

Hold the deck in the left hand, one side resting on second joints of second and third fingers, tip of thumb on top side, first and little fingers at opposite ends. Slip the thumb over the side so that its tip rests against the bottom card, and push it up and over on top, the card turning over in transit, so that if it were face down at bottom it will be face up on top.

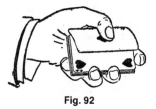

Fig. 92

(See Figs. 91 and 92.) The ends of the second, third and little fingers hold the deck in position as the card is pushed over, and the four finger ends unite in getting it squarely in place when on top.

The action should take place under cover of a short arm movement. Raise the hand up and in toward the person, and shift the position of the thumb just as the hand is about to make the down and outward movement, under which the action takes place. If one card is faced before it is exposed the deck will appear to be held face up, and the transferring of cards from the bottom may be continued to any desired extent. Though the process is very easy and can be performed with a motion too rapid to see, some little practice must be put in to acquire the knack of getting out the bottom card.

Both these one-hand transformations are much easier performed with about two-thirds of the deck.

BLIND SHUFFLES, RETAINING ENTIRE ORDER

In the first part of our book we described two blind shuffles for retaining either the upper or lower half of the deck in the same order, yet apparently shuffling the whole deck. Retaining the whole deck in a prearranged order is seldom or never attempted, or even desired, at the card table. But the conjurer performs many very interesting tricks through such an arrangement; therefore it is necessary to provide a blind shuffle that will not disturb any part of the deck. The following methods for retaining the entire order will be found sufficiently deceptive for his purpose, though by no means so perfect in appearance as the processes already described:

First Method. — Hold the deck in the left hand, crosswise, in the customary manner for the hand shuffle. Under-cut with the right hand about three-quarters of the deck, and bring it down in the usual way of shuffling on top of the packet in the left hand, dropping a small packet from the top. Now, in raising the right hand again, still in the ordinary manner, seize the lower packet that was first left in the left hand between the right third finger and thumb, bringing it up with the rest of the cards, the packet that was dropped from the top now falling against the left fingers, concealing the fact that the under packet is withdrawn. (See Fig. 93.) Now, with the left fingers tilt the packet over against the left thumb, and drop another small packet from the top of the right-hand portion

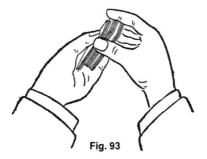

Fig. 93

into the left hand between its packet and the fingers, still with the usual movement for shuffling. The left thumb now tilts the packet back on the other, and the right hand makes its customary movement downward, but this time drops the lower packet that is held between the third finger and thumb, by simply releasing the pressure of the third finger. Now the left-hand portion is again tilted against the thumb, the right hand dropping another packet from the top, then the left-hand packet is tilted back, and the right hand throws the balance on top. This process leaves the order the same, the deck having received but a simple cut.

The right hand makes five up-and-down movements in the ordinary or regular manner of shuffling, and without hesitating for an instant. The left fingers and thumb keep up the process of tilting its portion back and forth, allowing the right-hand packets to fall above and below it. The actions of the right hand in bringing up the first packet from the left hand, with the first upward movement, and in releasing it again on the third downward movement (instead of dropping a packet from the top) are undetectable if the shuffle is performed with some degree of rapidity and smoothness. It is not at all difficult, but some practice is necessary.

The mode of shuffling over and under the left-hand packet is commonly employed, and incites no notice. The shuffle may be repeated as desired, and should be varied with an occasional cut.

Second Method. — This blind shuffle, or rather riffle, will require considerable practice to perform nicely, but it is worth it.

Seize the deck with both hands, face down, second and third fingers at one side, thumbs at the opposite side, little fingers at opposite ends, held somewhat under the deck, and first fingers curled in with tips on top. The second fingers touch each other at middle of side, and the thumbs touching at opposite side. Each hand occupies identically the same position. Now divide the pack with the thumbs and draw off the upper portion with the right hand; place the inner corners of the outer ends together so that the two packets form a sharp angle, but the right-hand packet about half an inch further out. Now riffle or spring the corners of the left-hand packet into the right-hand packet, both thumbs springing the cards, but beginning with the left thumb and finishing with the right, so that the left hand holds several cards that are not interwoven at the bottom, and about half a dozen of the right-hand packet are still free on top. (See Fig. 94.) Now shift the left hand slightly

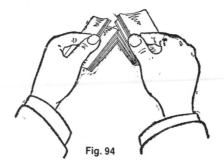

Fig. 94

so that the four fingers lie across the bottom of its packet, and with the right thumb spread the top cards fanwise over the left packet, at the same time bringing the inner ends of the two packets toward each other, twisting out the riffled upper corners and replacing the right-hand packet on top.

As the inner ends are brought together the two packets are spread somewhat, and the right little and third fingers twist out the bottom card first, and bend it in on top of the left-hand packet slightly in advance of the rest. This prevents any of the other cards going wrong. The more fanwise the packets are spread during the operation the more perfect the blind. The deck should be squared up rather slowly, the left thumb and fingers holding the deck with the cards in their irregular condition, the right hand being released and pushing or patting the cards into position. Care should be taken not to riffle the corners far into each other. The merest hold is sufficient, and in fact if the packets can be held under perfect control the cards need not be interlocked at all, and the difficulty of the twisting out process is avoided. By slightly spreading the two packets as the springing or riffling of the sides is continued the appearance of the corners being interlocked is perfectly maintained.

This shuffle can be performed very rapidly, and with perfect control of the cards, and it is an excellent one for conjuring, as these performers never riffle on the table. But, as we have mentioned, it is difficult, and if the operator is not a skillful card-handler he will find it quite a task to even riffle in the two packets, and this is the simplest part of the operation.

When this riffle is alternated with the foregoing shuffle it requires very close scrutiny of a very knowing card expert to detect the fact that the operation is a blind.

Third Method. — This is another form of the second method. The deck is seized with the thumbs and fingers at the ends instead of at the sides, the little fingers going under the sides, the positions being identical, only that the deck is turned endwise.

When the deck is separated into the two packets the thumbs riffle the inner corners together, the left fingers are shifted across the bottom, the right thumb spreads the top cards over the left-hand packet, and the right hand brings the outer ends of the two packets toward each other, twisting out the interlocked corners and placing the right-hand packet again on top in much the same manner.

In this method the packets are easier controlled, and it is hard to say which is the better. But we think for conjuring purposes the more the methods for blind shuffling are varied the greater are the probabilities of convincing the company that the cards are genuinely mixed; providing always, that the several methods employed appear the same as those in common every-day usage.

Fourth Method. — This is a very barefaced blind, simple, extremely easy, and surprisingly deceptive when cleverly performed.

Rest the deck on its side in the left hand in the usual position for shuffling, but hold the first finger against and along the end. Under-cut about half the deck with the right hand, the first finger on the top side, and make the ordinary movement to interlock or force the right-hand cards down among those in the left hand, bringing the sides together for that purpose. Allow a few of the cards from the top of the right-hand packet to drop down on top of the other packet, but prevent them from going quite to the left palm with the left thumb. Now keep up a constant lateral movement with the right hand, shifting the packet rapidly lengthwise about half an inch each way, as though forcing the two packets to interlace, but really dropping the upper cards on top of the left-hand packet, by holding the right-hand packet slightly diagonally over the lower one, so that the inner corner of the right-hand packet is just over the side of the lower one. Drop the top cards over in this manner until all are apparently interlocked about half way or more, then strike them on the top side with the fingers held flatly, driving them down even, and square up the deck.

The first finger held against the end and the first or top cards of the right-hand packet, going over immediately as the sides are brought together, effectually conceal the ruse. If the process of actually interlocking the cards is tried it will be seen how perfectly the action can be imitated. An occasional cut tends to increase the deception.

Fifth Method. — This process is very much employed by many clever card conjurers who ought to know better, and we include it only because it is in common use and to suggest its rejection. It consists in pushing small packets alternately from the top and bottom of the portion held in one hand to the bottom and top of the portion held in the other.

The deck is held in the left hand and several cards are pushed over by the left thumb into the right hand. Then the left fingers push several cards from the bottom on top of the right-hand cards. Then the left thumb again pushes several from the top, but these are received under the right-hand portion. The left fingers now push several from the bottom to the top of the right-hand portion, and so on until the left hand is empty.

This clumsy juggling might prove satisfactory if performed by an awkward novice before a parcel of school children, but it appears simply ridiculous in the hands of a card conjurer, who, it is presumed, knows how to shuffle a deck in the customary manner, and with at least the degree of smoothness that any ordinary person might possess.

METHODS FOR DETERMINING A CARD THOUGHT OF

In three of the following instances the spectator has no choice, as he is supposed to think of a card he sees, and the performer shows him but one, though apparently without design. In the fourth instance a most ingenious ruse is employed, the spectator being given perfect freedom, yet the card is determined almost as surely.

A. Hold the deck in the left hand, thumb across top near inner end, and first and second fingers at side. Bring over the right hand and seize deck with fingers at outer ends, thumb at inner end, and hold so that the outer ends of the cards may be sprung or "ruffled," with the faces towards the spectator. Requesting him to think of a card, spring the ends rapidly, stopping for an instant at any one place (see Fig. 95), then completing the ruffle. The springing is performed at such a pace that the spectator can recognize but one card, which is more fully exposed by the

Fig. 95

momentary lull in the springing, and at this point the performer forms and holds a break with end of left second finger. At the end of the first ruffle ask if card has been noted, and if not repeat the action, but of course hesitating at some other point.

B. Hold the deck lengthwise in the right hand, face to palm, between second joint of thumb and ends of fingers. Bend finger end downward and allow ends to escape rapidly, springing them into the left hand in the usual manner of the flourish. Hesitate, or stop the springing for an instant, at any stage of the operation (see Fig. 96), and the only card that the performer can notice or fairly distinguish will be the probable selection of the spectator. Of course the performer conceals his notice of the cards as far as possible.

C. Hold the deck across the left palm face down, extend it toward a spectator, requesting him to think of one of them. As he cannot see any he will naturally attempt to take the deck in his hands, or cut off a portion. In either case let him cut only, and the moment he sees the

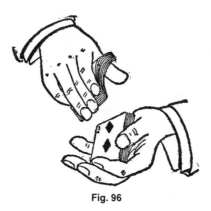

Fig. 96

bottom card of his packet thank him and take back the cut, holding a break at the location.

D. This cunning and absolutely unfathomable stratagem must have been devised by an individual of truly Machiavellian subtlety. The deck is held in the left hand face down and the cards are taken off in the right hand and held face to the spectator. Each card is counted as it is taken off the deck, and the right-hand packet is kept well squared up, so that but one card remains exposed to view. As the cards are exposed the hands are parted some little distance, and the action of drawing off the cards is made uniform, neither rapidly nor slowly. Now the operator looks covertly into the eyes of the spectator and he sees with surprising distinctness that they follow the movements of his right hand in taking off and exposing the cards. The moment the eyes rest, or lose their intensity, the performer notes the number of the card, but continues the drawing off process. Shortly, asking if a card has been thought of, he closes up deck, secretively counts off to the number, and produces at will. Of course a break may be held at the card noted, but the counting avoids the least change in the right-hand action.

TO GET SIGHT OF SELECTED CARD

A simple plan of catching a glimpse of a selected card is to have it inserted at the end and prevent the spectator from pushing it quite home by squeezing the deck. Then, with the card protruding about a quarter of an inch, covertly turn the deck partially over by passing it to the other hand, and get sight of the index.

Another and better plan is to push the selected card through diagonally, and square up, leaving it protruding at the inner end. In this case the index is at the diagonal corner and more easily seen, and the fact of the card protruding can be covered completely.

Still another plan is to insert the left little finger under the inserted card and slightly tilt up inner left-hand corner to note the index.

THE SLIDE

Hold the deck in the left hand, back to palm, fingers and thumb at opposite sides. Show face of deck to company, then turn it down, and with tips of third and little fingers slide the bottom card half an inch or so towards wrist (see Fig. 97), and draw the next card out at end with right-hand fingers. Of course this has the appearance of drawing off the card just shown to the company. It is a form of exchange that may be occasionally employed.

Fig. 97

FAVORITE SLEIGHTS FOR TERMINATING TRICKS

Catching Two Cards at Fingertips. — A favorite manner of terminating a trick that requires the production of two selected cards is to bring one to top and one to bottom, then toss the deck in the air a yard or so straight upward, retaining the top and bottom cards by pressure and friction of thumb and fingers, then thrusting the hand among the cards as they descend, apparently finding the selected cards in the act.

Leaving Selected Card in Hand of Spectator. — A plan for the production of a single card, as the last of a series, is to bring it to the bottom face up and request a spectator to hold the deck firmly by the corner, thumb on top. By striking the deck forcibly from above all the cards will fall from his hand save the selected card, which is retained by the friction of the fingers and left face up in his hand.

The Revolution. — This is a great favorite for terminating certain tricks, and has a very showy appearance. If the top card is pushed over the side about half an inch, and the deck dropped flatly on the table from a point of perhaps twelve or fifteen inches above it, the top card will turn over in the descent and lie fairly on top of the deck, face exposed. The turn is caused by the resistance of the air against the protruding side. The facts that the card to be produced is on top, and that a card is pushed over, are concealed.

Cards Rising from the Hand. — The selected cards are brought to top of deck and the pack is held in the left hand, thumb at one side and

Fig. 98

lying straight along with tip near end, second, third and little fingers at opposite side, and first finger at back. The cards are pushed up by first finger, the thumb and other fingers being released sufficiently to allow their rising, but retaining their position. (See Fig. 98.) When the cards are raised to nearly the full length the right hand takes them off. Some address is necessary to push up a card with one finger, but a little practice, and especially at the manner of holding the deck, so as to keep the card in position and yet not retard its upward course, will soon acquire the ability. If the first and second fingers are placed at the back the feat becomes much easier, but of course the effect is proportionately lessened.

CARD TRICKS

Explanatory. It is not our purpose to describe the various kinds of apparatus, or prepared or mechanical cards, that play so great a part in the professional conjurer's startling exhibitions. The enumeration alone of these devices would fill a volume twice this size; and anyway they would be of little service to the amateur for impromptu entertainment. But we shall describe some tricks that may be performed with an ordinary deck, under any circumstances, providing the necessary skill has been acquired to execute the sleights. However, the artist who has attained some degree of proficiency in manipulation as taught by this work, may by taxing his wits a little, devise no end of tricks for himself, with the advantage that they will not be "shop worn" articles.

The simplest sleight, if well rigged up with either plausible or nonsensical clap-trap, may be made to provide a most astonishing and elaborate card trick; whereas, if the sleight be exhibited alone, the effect is not at all commensurate with the time and labor spent in acquiring the skill. Conceal, as far as possible, the possession of digital ability, and leave the company still guessing how it is done.

For some of the following tricks we have invented names and garnished them up with a rigmarole merely to show the part that "patter" plays in card entertainments. Our readers essaying the tricks should compose their own monologue, so that it may be in keeping with their particular personality or style of address.

The Exclusive Coterie. — In Effect: The four Queens are selected and laid face down in a row on the table. Three indifferent cards are placed on each Queen. Now the company selects one of the four packets, and it is found to consist of the four Queens only.

Sleights: Palm and Shift.

Patter and Execution. — "Ladies and gentlemen, I shall endeavor to illustrate, with the aid of this ordinary deck of cards, how futile are the efforts of plebeians to break into that select circle of society known as the Beau-monde, and especially how such entree is prevented by the polite but frigid exclusiveness of its gentler members.

"We shall assume that it is the occasion of a public reception, our table the hall, our deck the common herd, and we may fittingly select the four Queens as representing the feminine portion of the Smart Set." (Lay four Queens face down on table.) "Will some one now kindly see that there are no more Queens in the deck." (Hand deck for inspection.) "There are no more Queens in the deck? Thanks!" (Take deck back.) "But are we all quite sure that the cards on the table are the four Queens? Please examine them." (Hand them to one of the company, and now secretly palm three cards in right hand.) "They are the four Queens? Kindly place them on the deck." (Extend deck in left hand and when Queens are placed on top secretly place palmed cards on top of them.) "Now, as our table is supposed to be the scene of this grand function, we shall station those four particularly exclusive ladies at different points in the room" (lay out the first three top cards face down), "giving her majesty the Queen of —— " (hesitate and carelessly turn Queen face up apparently to see the suit, and allow the company to see it also, then name the suit), "the post of honor near the entrance." (Lay first Queen on the table and make a shift, holding location of other three Queens.) "Now, as would naturally be the case, we shall besiege these high strung patrician ladies with attentions from the lower orders, which the rest of the deck represents, by first surrounding her majesty on the right with three cards from the top" (lay three cards on first table card), "and to show no partiality we shall cut the deck haphazard, and plague our second liege lady with three of the first presumptuous plebeians we may find there" (cut off small packet and place three cards on second table card), "and though the proximity or even notice of any of these common persons are equally abhorrent to our grand dames we shall treat them all alike by again cutting and surrounding her majesty at the entrance with three more rank outsiders" (this time cut to location of shift, and place the three Queens on table Queen), "and permit three more from the bottom who have been least crowding and therefore more deserving to proffer their homage to the other fair one." (Lay three bottom cards on the other table card.)

"Now, ladies and gentlemen, as you have seen, I have brutally taken advantage of these unprotected and tenderly nurtured creatures by placing them in circumstances that must be extremely galling to their aristocratic sensibilities. Will they endure such conditions? Having some knowledge of the marvelous subtlety, finesse and resources of the sex, I feel confident they can, with tact and discretion, easily elude their persecutors, and form a more congenial coterie among themselves. Will some one please select two of these packets?" (Whichever packets are selected place those two that do not contain the Queens at the back of the table side by side.) "Thanks. Now kindly tell me which of the two remaining packets I shall take?" (In any case pick up the two packets, placing the Queens at the front of the table and the second packet back beside the others. The question is purposely ambiguous.)

"Now we must see whether I were over-confident in predicting that the Queens would seek each other's society. If they are all found in one packet I was right. In which packet would they be most likely to congregate? As the front packet was your selection, and as it is given the most prominent position, I think the fatal vanity of the sex would tempt them to be there. We shall see." (Turn up four Queens, then face the other three packets, showing no Queens among them.)

It will have been seen by the foregoing that the presentation of a card trick may contain much more bosh than action, and indeed the performance of the one just described might be advantageously prolonged by a great deal more nonsense. In all card entertainments the more palaver the more the interest is excited, and the address and patter of the performer will count as much if not more than his skill in manipulation.

The Divining Rod. — In Effect: A card is freely selected by the company and replaced in the pack, which is thoroughly shuffled. The performer is now blindfolded, shuffles the cards in this condition, then spreads them face down over the table, poises a pen-knife over the mass, and suddenly pierces the selected card through with the open blade.

Sleights: Shift, Palm and Blind Shuffle.

Execution and Patter. — "Ladies and gentlemen. It is a fact well known to archaeologists that many very wonderful arts which were possessed by the ancients have, through the course of ages, been completely lost to modern civilization. Prominent among these superior accomplishments was the mysterious power of divining the presence of water or metals that lay hidden far under the ground. Now it may be that the assertion I am about to make will be received by you with polite but none the less absolute incredulity; but it has been my very great good fortune to discover, by the merest accident, the underlying principle of this lost art, and I have mapped out a plan of experiment and study that will in time, I trust, enable me to give once more to the world complete and scientific data for positively ascertaining the immediate whereabouts of such metals as gold, silver or copper by a process as simple as the waving of a willow wand over the prospected area.

"I do not myself as yet fully understand the exact nature of the power I have stumbled upon, but I know it to be a sort of magnetic or sympathetic attraction, and I shall illustrate to you the principle involved by experimenting with a deck of cards. Will some one please make a selection of one card? Thank you. Now I wish you to remember the name. Put it back anywhere in the deck." (Shift and palm off card.) "Would you like to shuffle? Mix them up thoroughly." (Take back deck, placing palmed card on top and show large handkerchief.) "Now, ladies and gentlemen, although no ordinary power on earth can find that selected card, I am going to satisfy all present that it is a very extraordinary power indeed that will assist me in producing it. As a matter of fact, the power is entirely apart from any personal ability I may possess; the merit of the feat will be solely due to the mysterious properties of this little pen-knife. To conclusively prove that I take no part in the action I shall have some one blindfold me with this handkerchief." (Fold the handkerchief, and when it is being knotted at back adjust fold over eyes and nose so that table can be seen when looking straight downward.) "Now, as it is utterly impossible for me to see at all, I shall again shuffle the cards" (blind shuffle and leave one extra card on top), "and spread them out over the table." (Spread the deck on the table with a rotary motion, gradually working off top card and retaining second card with finger or thumb, employing both hands so that selected card can be almost wholly covered. Keep exposed corner in sight and spread balance of cards still further over table. Now take open pen-knife in hand.) "Please observe that I do not touch the cards at all." (Poise knife daintily between finger and thumb, circle about with hovering motion, and suddenly pierce card through its exposed part. Remove handkerchief, request name of card and slowly turn it up on point of blade.)

We consider this trick a capital one if performed with some address. Of course the patter is all a matter of taste and any invention may answer. The possibility of getting a perfect view of the table when the eyes are bandaged is never suspected by the uninitiated, but it is a fact well known to conjurers. The slightest glint is quite sufficient, as the head may be moved about freely so as to take in the whole plane below. Under any circumstances it is difficult to fold a handkerchief so that no ray of light will enter from beneath.

This trick may be performed without getting sight of the card, by retaining the selected card under finger of one hand and then the other, and when spreading is complete retaining its position well exposed, and piercing by mechanical judgment of its location.

The Invisible Flight. — In Effect: A card is selected by the company. The performer places it on the table to the right. Another card is selected and performer places it on table to the left. The first drawn card is now placed on top of the deck, which was lying on the table, and the two selected cards are commanded to change places and found to have done so.

Sleights: Top Change and Palm Change.

Execution: Stand behind the table facing the company. Have a card selected by a spectator to the right, hold deck in left hand, take back drawn card in right hand, show it first to the company on the right, then to company on the left, then exchange it for top card of deck when making half turn again to the right and deposit card with same movement on the table at the right side. Now have the second card selected by some spectator to the left, palm the top card in right hand when closing the deck, and hold deck in right hand by ends, face down. Take back second drawn card in left hand, showing it to company on left. Now drop deck on middle of table, and take second selected card from the left hand into the right, seizing it by the ends, and depositing palmed card on top of it. Hold closely together and show as one card to company on the right. The right hand now contains the two selected cards. Make "Palm Change," taking first selected card in left hand, and deposit it on left side of table. Immediately pick up card on right side of table by ends, with the right hand, and drop it openly from several inches above, on top of deck. Pick up deck by drawing it with sliding movement to edge of table, depositing palmed card on top, and place the pack on the table to the right. As the exchange is now made finish the trick as desired.

The first exchange is made by employing the "Top Change," and the tacit excuse for bringing the hands together for the instant is obtained by showing the card first to the company on the right, then to the left, and then depositing the card on right side of table. The second exchange is made very slowly, or at least in the usual time required to pass a card from one hand to the other. The entire company should be permitted to see the card about to be palmed; then the hand is naturally turned down as the left fingers apparently carry away to the left the card just shown. When the table card is dropped on the deck, it may be permitted to fall unevenly, giving one reason for picking up the deck, i. e., to square up. Transferring the deck from the middle of the table to the right side is the second tacit excuse.

This trick is usually performed by having one duplicate card, and forcing it, in which case the assistance of the deck for the third exchange is not required. But as we confine our list to those that may be performed with an ordinary deck, the foregoing method will be found satisfactory.

TRICKS WITH THE PREARRANGED DECK

The usual plan is to arrange the whole pack in the order suggested by the following jingle, viz.:

"Eight Kings threatened to save
Ninety-five Queens from one sick Knave."

Thus indicating the order of the thirteen values, as Eight, King, Three, Ten, Two, Seven, Nine, Five, Queen, Four, Ace, Six, Jack. The suits are taken in a regular order, say, Diamonds, Clubs, Hearts, Spades. To arrange the deck, lay the Eight of Diamonds face up on the table, then place the King of Clubs face up on that, then the Three of Hearts on that, then Ten of Spades, Two of Diamonds, Seven of Clubs, Nine of Hearts, Five of Spades, Queen of Diamonds, and so on, continuing until the fifty-two cards are laid out, the last card being the Jack of Spades.

Any arrangement is as good as another so long as the values do not run in their regular order, i. e., One, Two, Three, Four, Five, etc., and though the above arrangement is well known, it does not matter in the least when performing. Only those who are well versed in card tricks would recognize the order, and such persons cannot be deceived with any kind of arrangement. The tax on the memory is very slight, there being but thirteen names to commit, and conning them over for half an hour or so should impress their order on the mind permanently. The deck so arranged makes every thirteenth card the same value, and of the next suit in the order of suits; every fourth card the same suit, and every second card the other suit of the same color.

Cutting does not disturb the order and the top card is always next in the regular order to the bottom, and the performer, secretly noting the bottom card, has the key to the situation. We shall describe several very startling effects that may be caused by the employment of the prearranged deck in the hands of a really clever operator.

Of course, the prearrangement must be carefully concealed. The performer first blind shuffles, then requests some spectator to cut. Then spreading the cards fanwise with both hands, requests the spectator to select any number of the cards, and permits him to do so but from only one position in the fan, withdrawing the deck immediately as the cards are drawn, so as to prevent any attempt to select from different positions. The performer now separates his hands and the deck, at the point where the cards were drawn, and the right hand carelessly places the cards which were above those drawn, under the left-hand portion. He now secretly notes the bottom card, barely sighting the index at the base of the left thumb, then raises the inner corner of the top card slightly with the left thumb, getting a glimpse of its index. There is little or no fear of the action being noticed, as the company is not yet informed of the nature of the trick, and the principal attention is taken by the cards selected. The performer may now finish the trick in any manner. He has learned the number of cards drawn, and what cards they are, by naming over mentally in the prearranged order, beginning from the bottom card that he has noted, the cards that should be between it and the top card, which he has also noted. He may first pretend to determine the number drawn by weighing those that are left, and then take back the selected cards one at a time, boldly proclaiming that though the difference in the weight of each card is infinitely little, still there is a difference; and delicately ascertaining its suit and value by this means as he holds it poised in the right hand. Or he may assume the power of mind-reading, determining first the color then the suit, then the value of each card. Or he may terminate the trick by simply naming the cards in their order. There are a hundred and one variations, and in carrying them out the performer must see that the arranged order is not disturbed, so that he may continue his experiments with the deck. There is no reason that he should not look at the cards when they are returned, but they are rarely changed from the order drawn.

The performer may now request the company to call for any particular card, and he can locate it almost instantly from his knowledge of the bottom card, and he makes the two-handed shift, bringing it into view. He may hold the deck face up in the left hand, and slightly spring the outer corners under cover of the right hand, glancing at the index; or hold it face down and spring the inner corners. In either event he has only thirteen cards to run through before finding one of the same value as that called for, and if the suit is not the same it instantly tells him that it must be the thirteenth, or twenty-sixth card from the one found.

The performer may, of course, name every card in the deck, taking them off one at a time and calling the value and suit before he throws it face up on the table; but rather than make the trick so long, and such a constant repetition, it is preferable to name half a dozen or so, then execute a blind shuffle, have the deck cut again, and begin once more. By assuming to determine the value and suit by the sense of smell, or any chicanery, is more misleading, and has a better effect.

But the most remarkable feats that may be accomplished with the prearranged deck have yet to be described. The performer executes a blind shuffle thoroughly, requests a spectator to cut, and lays the deck face down on the table. Now some member of the company is requested to give any number between one and fifty-two, and the performer immediately names the card that will be found at that number. When this has been verified, and the shuffle and cut are again made, the performer lays the deck on the table and this time desires the company to give the name of any card in the pack. The performer at once calls the number at which it will be found, and proves his accuracy by slowly and openly counting the cards until it is reached. Of course, in each instance the performer has noted the bottom card after the cut was made, and before he placed the deck on the table. We have formulated the following rules for determining the card that will be found at the number given, and for ascertaining the number at which any particular card called for will be located.

To determine the card that is at any particular number, its suit is first determined. Divide the number by four, and if there is no remainder the suit is the same as the bottom card. If the remainder is one, the suit is the next in the order of suits. If the remainder is two, the suit is the second in the order of suits, or the other suit of the same color. If the remainder is three, the suit is the third in the order of suits, or the preceding suit, always calculating from the suit of the bottom card.

Now having ascertained the suit of the card at the number given, we proceed to learn its value. First divide the number by thirteen. If there is no remainder, the value is the same as the bottom card; but this is very improbable. If there is a remainder, name over mentally in the arranged order, as many cards as the remainder, beginning with the top card (which is next in order to the bottom), and the last card mentally named will denote the value of the card at the number given. Then the value and suit, or the name of the card at the number, is proclaimed to the company and the prediction verified.

To ascertain the number at which any particular card called for will be found, we first determine where the first card of that value is, and the suit of that first card. To find the number at which this first card of like value is located, mentally name over the arranged order, starting with the top card (which is next in order to the bottom) until the card of like value is reached. Of course, the number will be less than thirteen. Then find the suit of this card by dividing its number by four, as explained in the first rule. Now if the suit chances to be the suit of the card called for, the task is completed, but the odds are three to one against it. If the required suit is the next in the order of suits, add thirteen to the first number. If the suit required is the second in the order, add twenty-six to the first number; and if the suit of the card called for is the third in the order of suits, or the preceding suit, add thirty-nine to the first number, and in each instance it will be the number at which the card called for will be found.

We shall first give an example of determining the card that will be found at any particular number. Assume that the company gives the number thirty-five, and the bottom card is the King of Spades. Following the rule, we divide the number thirty-five by four, and get a remainder of three. This gives us the suit as the third in order from the bottom suit, or the preceding suit which is Hearts. Now to determine the value of the thirty-fifth card. The rule is "divide the number by thirteen," and this gives us a remainder of nine. Now we mentally name our nine cards in their order, from the King at the bottom: "Three, Ten, Two, Seven, Nine, Four, Queen, Four, Ace." The Ace being the ninth card determines the value. Hence the thirty-fifth card is the Ace of Hearts.

Dividing any number under fifty-two by thirteen is very simple; remembering that it goes evenly into thirteen, twenty-six, and thirty-nine, the remainder can be instantly calculated. When mentally running over the order, the values only are rehearsed, thereby taking half the time that would be required to rehearse both value and suit of each card. The suit having been obtained by the first division by four, only the value remains to be determined. A clever performer can name the card almost instantly.

As an example of determining the number at which any particular card will be found, we shall assume the company calls for the Ten of Diamonds, and the bottom card is the Six of Clubs. The rule is to "first, determine where the first card of the same value is, and the suit of that card." We mentally rehearse the order from the Six at the bottom until we reach the first Ten, viz.: "Jack, Eight, King, Three, Ten," finding the first Ten is the fifth card. Now to learn its suit, we divide by four, getting the remainder of one. This gives us the suit as the first in order from the bottom card. As the bottom card is a Club, the Ten located is a Heart. Now, as the card called for is the Ten of Diamonds, and Diamonds is the second suit from Hearts, we apply the rule and add twenty-six to the first number found (five), and get thirty-one, which is the number at which the Ten of Diamonds will be found.

The card conjurer's repertory is never complete without employing the prearranged deck to some extent, and we believe the rules here given for determining the card at any number given, and the number of any card called for, are the first ever formulated for a fifty-two-card deck.

The Traveling Cards. — In Effect: A card is selected and replaced in the deck, which is then thoroughly shuffled. Performer now causes the cards to fly up his sleeve, one, two, or several at a time, producing them from the shoulder. The selected card is called upon to leave the deck at the company's desire, and the operation is continued until the last several cards, which are noted, disappear from the hand and are slowly produced from the shoulder.

Sleights: Masterly feats of Palming and Unflinching Audacity.

Execution and Patter: "Ladies and gentlemen: I am constantly importuned by some of the most curious and least discerning of my auditors to explain the manner by which the results in certain tricks are achieved. While I consider it unprofessional to make these disclosures, I accede somewhat to the prevalent demand, and to-night I am going to take you especially into my confidence and expose one of the most important secrets in the whole realm of conjuring. Although many professors of the art vehemently deny the imputation, it is nevertheless a fact that the coat sleeve of the magician is to him much the same as a Saratoga trunk to a summer girl. Where does he get his bouquets of roses, baskets of eggs, dishes of swimming fishes? 'Up his sleeve.' How do his rabbits, bird cages and cannon balls disappear? 'Up his sleeve.' The saying is as true as it is ancient, and I shall prove my assertions by demonstrating the process; and though you may doubt my veracity, you certainly cannot question your own eyes.

"As a preliminary, I wish some one to kindly oblige by selecting a card from the deck. Any one you wish. Now please remember the name and place it again in the deck." (Card is inserted, shifted and palmed.) "Will you shuffle for me?" (Deck is shuffled and returned. Place palmed card on top and palm off eight or ten more with it in right hand, hold deck in left.) "Now to illustrate the point in question, ladies and gentlemen, I am going to cause these cards to fly up my sleeve and out through the armhole here." (Indicate place by thrusting the right hand into the shoulder of coat, and leave palmed cards there.) "Now, attention, please, and you may see them fly, or if you do not see them, you may hear them. First card, go!" (Click corner of deck with left little finger, carelessly show right hand empty, passing it rather quickly under coat to shoulder and produce bottom card. Show it and throw on table.) "Well, you see the first card obeyed me. Second card, pass!" (Produce another from bottom.) "Third card!" (Produce; each time clicking deck with finger as cards are ordered to pass, and showing cards as produced.) "But we have had a card selected and shuffled in the deck, and though we have no idea where it is I shall command it to fly up my sleeve at whatever number you may elect. What shall it be — four, five, six or seven? The sixth? Very well. As three cards have already passed, the selected card shall be the third one. Pass!" (Produce.) "Pass!" (Produce.) "Oh, what is the name of the card you selected? Jack of Hearts! Well, Jack of Hearts, it is your turn, sir. You will please oblige the company by flying up my sleeve." (Produce top card, showing it to be the one called upon.) "To show the ease with which the cards travel I shall order several to pass together." (Palm eight or ten in left hand from bottom.) "I have only to speak a little louder. Pass!" (Take deck in right hand and thrust left into right shoulder, withdrawing two or three of the palmed cards, leaving balance there.) "You see, I have three cards this time, and they travel equally well through either sleeve. Go! Four cards passed. Go! Three cards. It may be thought that I have duplicate cards concealed in my coat above, but that is easily disproved. You see there are no cards there. (Throw open fully right side of coat, from which all cards have been taken, and left side partially.) "Besides, if you watch the deck you will notice that it is gradually growing less. To save time I shall hasten their activity. Go!" (Take deck again in left hand and produce balance in left shoulder, then palm again in left hand.) "Three cards that time. Pass!"

(Thrust palmed cards in right shoulder and produce about half of them, then palm from top with right hand.) "Five that time. Go!" (Produce half with right hand, leaving balance.) "Four. Pass!" (Produce balance from left shoulder.) "Five cards. Pass!" (Change hands and produce balance from right shoulder.) "Now, how many have we left — one, two, three, four, five, six. Six only. Please note what they are. The King, Trey, Seven, Ten, Ace, and another Seven. Shall I pass them all at once, or one at a time? All together? Very well. Now, all of you, be gone!" (Bring left hand down below right, then when repassing right with quick outward movement propel cards into right palm with left first finger, making snapping noise, point right index finger at empty left hand for instant, then thrust right into left shoulder and slowly produce, showing cards are same as named.)

Although this trick is one of the oldest, it is one of the prettiest; and in the hands of a really clever artist never fails in producing a most pleasing and brilliant effect. Some performers produce the cards from the bosom beneath the vest, but we think the shoulder preferable. The cards can be slipped partially into the coat sleeve near top of shoulder, and their position securely maintained while the arms are moved about at will. The hand that holds the deck should be extended as the cards are commanded to pass. Using both sleeves gives excuse for changing deck from hand to hand, creating favorable and natural opportunities for palming, and also preventing the spectators anticipating which hand will produce the cards until it is too late.

The Row of Ten Cards. — In Effect: The performer shuffles the deck and lays the first ten cards face down in a row on the table. The performer now turns away while any number of the cards are transferred from one end to the other. Then, without having seen the action, or being aided in any manner, the performer immediately turns up one card whose value indicates the number of cards that were transferred; permitting this action to be repeated as often as desired, and determining the number moved each time.

Execution: Arrange ten cards in consecutive order from Ace to Ten, and place on top of deck, the Ten being uppermost. Blind shuffle and lay out the ten cards face down in a row on the table, begining at the left, so that the Ten is the left end card of the row. Explain to company that any number may be transferred from the right to the left end. As the order must be maintained, it is well to insist that but one card must be moved at a time. This will preserve the order, and not be likely to impress the company that there is any certain arrangement.

The rules for determining the number transferred from right to left are, first: The left end card will always indicate the number of the first transfer: i. e., when the first transfer of any number of cards is made, the value or number of spots of the card at the left end will be the number of the cards that were transferred; so that by turning up the left end card when the first move is made, the performer indicates the number that were transferred. On the second or any subsequent transfer, the card to turn is determined by adding the value, or number of spots, of the last card turned, to the number of the place it occupies in the row.

For example, the cards, when first laid out, will stand:

Ten, Nine, Eight, Seven, Six, Five, Four, Three, Two, One. Assume the company transfer four cards, the order will then be:

Four, Three, Two, One, Ten, Nine, Eight, Seven, Six, Five, so that when the rule for determining the first transfer is applied, and the left end card turned, it would indicate that four cards were transferred.

When the card is turned the calculation for determining the next transfer is at once made by the second rule, "adding the value of the card turned (four) to the number of its place in the row" (one), making five. When the next transfer is made the fifth card is turned and it indicates the number transferred. Let us prove this by assuming that two cards are now transferred. The new order will be:

Six, Five, Four, Three, Two, One, Ten, Nine, Eight, Seven. Now, counting from the left, we turn the fifth card in the row, and find the Two, indicating the number transferred. Again add the number of turned card (two) to its place in the row (five), and we get seven, which will be the number in the row to turn, when the next transfer is made.

Of course, if this is continued, the number will in time be greater than ten; in which case ten is subtracted from the number, and the remainder indicates the position of the card to turn.

If the company should test the performer's ability by making no transfer, or by transferring the ten cards, the card turned will always be the Ten; and in such case the performer will at once state that transferring all or none was not a part of the conditions made, thus concealing the fact that he cannot tell whether all or none were moved.

The first move should always be made by the performer when explaining the experiment to the company, and thereby avoid turning up the end card. As the performer makes the first transfer, he simply adds one to the number moved, one being the position of the card that otherwise would be turned, and he has the position for the turn when the company makes the first transfer.

Much effect may be obtained with this trick if the proper address and by-play are indulged. The performer may affect to accomplish the feat by mind reading, and increase the interest by failing to fathom the subtlety of some lady's intellectual faculty, and easily wresting the secret from the coarser calibre of some gentleman, even against his will; and by pretending to have determined the number transferred before turning the card, and making the finding of the particular card also dependent upon some extraordinary power.

The trick is one of the very best of those not requiring sleight of hand.

The Acrobatic Jacks. — In effect: The Jacks are placed by the company at top, bottom, and middle of the deck, and keep constantly changing positions in most remarkable manner.

Sleights: One- and Two-Hand Shifts.

Patter and Execution: "Ladies and gentlemen: You have all doubtless been interested or amused, at one time or another, by the remarkable performances of educated animals. The dog, the pony, the elephant, and even the pig, have all been carefully trained to understand and obey each word or sign of their masters. But have you ever witnessed the performance of an educated pack of cards? You do not know that cards can be educated? I assure you that it is quite possible, and I shall demonstrate the truth of my assertion. Moreover, I have discovered in my efforts to educate my fifty-two pupils, that they, like the members of any other family, possess certain individual characteristics or temperaments, and I have endeavored to develop the special talents of each, in the direction most in keeping with the natural bent.

"I shall select the four Jacks for the purpose of illustrating how an original athletic tendency that was early manifested by them has been developed by a system of training, until they have acquired a degree of skill in acrobatic feats that is truly remarkable. I wish two ladies or gentlemen in the audience to assist me, by each holding two of the Jacks." (Give two red Jacks to spectator, whom we shall designate as A., and two black Jacks to second spectator, whom we shall call B. Then to A.) "Will you, sir, place one of the red Jacks on top of the deck? Thank you. And will you (to B.) place one of the black Jacks in the middle of the deck?" (Open pack with left thumb bookwise, ready for the "Charlier Pass," and when Jack is inserted shift packets.)

"Now, ladies and gentlemen, we have a red Jack on top, and a black Jack in the middle, and as a first display of their intelligence and training, I shall order them to change places. Ready. Go!" (Click deck with little finger and show change has taken place. Hand Jacks back to A. and B.) "You see that they are quite active and very obedient. We shall try them again and place them farther apart. (To A.) Place your red Jack at the bottom. (To B.) Place your black Jack on top. Now observe, I shall not touch the cards," (Make gesture with the right hand as if to show that this hand would be the one necessarily employed, and as attention is attracted to it, shift with the left.) "but shall command the Jacks to perform a somersault from the top and bottom and meet in the middle.

Attention. Go!" (Click deck, show top and bottom cards, then show Jacks in middle. Close deck with little finger between Jacks, and shift with both hands.) "That was a forward somersault, ladies and gentlemen, but they perform backwards just as easily. I shall show you. Ready. Go!" (Click deck and show Jacks again at top and bottom.)

"I trust I have impressed you somewhat with the intelligence and agility the Jacks possess in themselves, but for fear you may fancy that I have anything to do with their performance, I shall call upon all four Jacks to execute their grand and lofty tumbling at the same time, and I need not say to you, ladies and gentlemen, that however clever I might be, I could not possibly, of my own power, instantaneously change the positions of four cards at four different points." (Give back Jacks to A. and B., and have A. place his at top and bottom, and B. place his two in middle. Insert little finger between middle Jacks and make shift with both hands.) "Now, please remember the order. The two red Jacks are at the top and bottom, and the two black Jacks are in the middle. This time I shall order the four to play leap-frog, and each take the place of the other. Ready. Go!" (Make click and show the changes have taken place.)

"I cannot doubt, after this demonstration, that you are quite satisfied the Jacks have been fairly well trained; and I am now going to make them perform their acrobatic feat very slowly, so that you may all see just how it is done." (Give back Jacks to A. and B. Then to A.) "Place your two red Jacks again at the top and bottom;" (then to B.) "and now we shall have yours again in the middle. But stop! On second thought, as you are to see how it is done, I shall have the Jacks execute their somersaults while the deck is in your hands. I assure you they will perform equally well, and the moment you place your cards in the middle I wish you to hold the deck yourself." (Apparently cut deck in the middle, but really make two-handed shift without bringing the two packets together again, holding the right-hand packet a few inches over the left when shift is made. Have Jacks placed between, and immediately close packets, putting deck in B.'s hands.) "Now, sir, don't hold them too firmly, and watch them perform. I shall order all four to come together at the middle. All ready. Go! Did you see them go? Nor even feel them go? That is strange, for they certainly obeyed me. Look at the top and bottom cards. They have gone! Now look in the middle and you will find them all together as commanded."

A *Mind-Reading Trick.* — Sleights: Stock Shuffle.

Execution and Patter: "Ladies and gentlemen, I shall next attempt an experiment in mind-reading, and though I do not claim to be an adept in the art, I have managed to obtain an understanding of its fundamental principles, and I shall endeavor to demonstrate that under favorable conditions I can actually read the thought that is most prominent in the mind of a willing subject. I wish some gentleman in the audience who is desirous of giving my ability a fair and impartial test, to take this deck of cards in his own hands and select any four he may wish for the purpose of my experiment." (Give deck to spectator, who selects four cards at will, and take back deck.) "Now, sir, will you please make a mental note of any one card of the four you have selected, and as an aid to impress it most firmly, think of the one that to you may appear the most easily remembered. If you can associate one of them with a prominent date, or some incident in your own life, so much the better; and, if possible, disabuse your mind completely of the other three. Have you done this? Thank you. Now insert the four anywhere in the deck." (Have cards replaced in middle, form break above, with right thumb at inner end, turn on side in left hand in position for blind shuffle. Under-cut to about half portion above break, shuffle off to break, run two, in-jog running, say, seventeen, out-jog and shuffle off. Under-cut to in-jog and throw on top. Under-cut to out-jog, run seven and throw balance on top. This action places two of the selected cards the ninth and tenth from the top, and the other two the eighteenth and nineteenth.) "Now, ladies and gentlemen, I have doubtless quite satisfied you, and most certainly myself, that the four cards drawn, including the particular one thought of, are hopelessly lost in the shuffle; but before attempting to read the mind of the gentleman who is so kindly assisting me in the experiment, I wish to be assured that he has got the card firmly established in his memory. Please watch these cards as I expose them. I shall not attempt to determine the card should it appear, by any outward sign you may make; in fact, I shall not look at either you or the cards." (Expose seventeen cards, one at a time, throwing them carelessly one on the other, face up, on the table. Note the two selected cards, the ninth and tenth, as they fall on the table, paying no attention to the others.) "Did you see the cards you thought of?" (If he did, it is one of those noted. If not, it is one of the next two selected cards, which are now on top of deck. In either event:) "Well, I see that you are not at all uncertain about your memory." (Now assuming the thought card is on the table; if they are of different color, by ascertaining the color of the thought card, its identity is established. If of the same color, but different suit, the suit will fix its identity. If both color and suit are the same, the value must be different, and the first question is asked concerning the point of difference. In whichever particular they differ, color preferred, gaze intently into the individual's eyes.) "Please think of the color. Was it red?" (In event of it being so, it will be presumed that the guess was certain knowledge. Should he answer "No," step close to him, taking his hand.)

"Kindly permit me to come in contact with you, and I am certain to obtain a perfect impression of your thought." (In either event the answer to the first question discloses the identity of the thought card.) "Oh, now I obtain a startlingly clear impression of the color, and the suit is Diamonds." (Or, as the case may be.) "Now, please think solely of the value." (Then, meditatively.) "Was it a Court or a Spot card? Now, as I close my eyes to prevent the confusion of external objects, I see it is covered with spots; one, two, three, four, five, six, seven. Yes, it is the Seven of Diamonds." (Or, as the case may be.)

Should the thought card not have been one of those exposed, and the chances are even, get a glimpse of the two top cards when replacing the table cards, or by shifting them to the bottom, and proceed in the same manner to ascertain which is the one thought of.

Power of Concentrated Thought. — In Effect: A spectator is requested to think of a card. Performer now lays deck on the table and requests another spectator to think of a number. Both spectators are now requested to whisper the name and number to each other, and mentally command the card thought of to take its position in the deck at the number thought of. The performer, who has not been near the deck in the interim, now requests the name and number, and permits a spectator to take the deck in hand and ascertain for the company that the silent injunction has been obeyed.

Execution: When requesting the first spectator to think of a card, employ one of the several methods given for "Determining the Card Thought Of." Bring this card to the top. Secretly count seven cards at bottom and shift to top. Lay deck on the table, and request second spectator to "think of a number between one and ten." The trick is based on the very strong probability that he will think of seven. Now babble nonsense about the power of concentrated thought upon even inanimate objects, requesting parties to whisper name and number, and mentally urge the required action. Now request name and number. If the number is seven, tell him to count off the number thought of, and turn the next card. If the number is eight, tell him to turn the card at the number thought of. However, should the number be more or less than either, the performer must pick up the deck himself, and when handing it to the spectator shift one from the bottom if the number is nine, or the requisite number from the top if less than seven. But the chances are ten to one that seven will be the number thought of.

The Acme of Control. — In Effect: A spectator selects two cards. Then takes the deck in his own hands, inserts the cards himself, shuffles to any extent, and returns deck to performer, who produces the selected cards instantly.

Sleights: Force and Palm.

Execution: Secretly place Five of Diamonds and Four of Hearts, at top or bottom of deck, and Four of Diamonds and Five of Hearts, in middle. Force the two middle cards on spectator, palm the other two when closing deck, and immediately hand the pack to spectator, telling him to insert the drawn cards and shuffle. Give him as little time as possible to meditate on his selection, as the trick is based on the similarity of the forced cards and the palmed ones. When the deck is returned, finish the trick as desired, and when producing the two palmed cards, boldly proclaim them as the ones drawn. If the trick be performed properly, not one in fifty will discover the imposition unless in the secret. The difference between the cards forced, and the cards produced, is so little remarkable that it is seldom or never detected. The Sevens and Eights, or the Deuces and Treys, or any two pairs of the spot cards of the same color, would probably answer as well.

The performer may engage to cause the selected cards to appear together at top, or bottom, or middle of deck, at the option of the company, and shift the palmed cards to such position as decided upon; or he may "pass" the cards under some object on the table, or to the pocket of a spectator, in which latter events he will have secretly placed the cards there beforehand instead of on top or bottom of deck.

The Card and Handkerchief. — In Effect: A card is freely selected, restored to the deck and thoroughly shuffled. The deck is now wrapped up in a borrowed handkerchief, which is held suspended by the corners,

Fig. 99

and upon command the selected card is seen to slowly project itself through the handkerchief and flutter to the floor.

Execution: Borrow a rather large handkerchief first. Place it in full sight in vest or on table, then have card selected and replaced in deck, shift to top, palming in right hand, and return deck to be shuffled. Now take corner of handkerchief in each hand, show both sides by crossing right hand over left, keeping right palm to person, then throw handkerchief over right palm, one corner lying along right arm, and diagonal corner hanging down over right fingers the hand being about the middle. Now take back deck with left hand and place it on hand-

Fig. 100

kerchief lengthwise over right hand, seizing it by ends with that hand, and squaring up palmed card against it, at same time taking out the crimp so that it will lie flatly. Then, with the left hand, bring up the overhanging corner of handkerchief, covering the deck, and showing the right-hand fingers; seize sides of deck with left hand, gather back the folds of handkerchief with right so that the selected card will be retained at its inner end and suspend the deck by the folds with the right hand, holding well above the pack. (See Figs. 99 and 100.) Now command the selected card to appear, first requesting the drawer to give its name, and by giving slight up-and-down jolts to the deck, the card will slowly emerge from the back, having all the appearance of forcing its way through the center of the handkerchief at the lower end of the suspended deck.

The Top and Bottom Production. — In Effect: Four persons freely select two cards each. All are restored to the deck, which is thoroughly shuffled. The top and bottom cards are now shown not to be any of those selected. The performer then causes the several pairs to instantly appear at top and bottom as called for.

Sleights: Two-Handed Shift, Palm and Blind Shuffle.

Execution and Patter: "Ladies and gentlemen: For the purpose of this experiment, I shall request several individuals in the company to each select two cards. I wish you to take particular note of those you draw so that you will know them again." (Allow four persons, whom we shall call A., B., C. and D., to freely select two cards each. When all are selected, take them back in the reverse order, saying to D.) "Will you kindly place your two in the deck?" (When this is done, shift, palm off, and hand deck to be shuffled. Take back deck, replace palmed cards on top, turn to C.) "Please place your two in the middle." (Shift without closing two packets, appearing as a simple cut, and have C.'s cards now placed on D.'s. Again shift to top, and execute blind shuffle, jogging first card, and leaving selected cards in the middle. Now cut to, and include jog card, and have B.'s cards placed on first two pairs. Repeat the action taken last and have A.'s cards replaced in same manner, then shift and blind shuffle, and run three extra cards on top of the four pairs which are now on top of the pack.)

"Now, ladies and gentlemen, we have had eight cards selected by four of you, and all have been thoroughly shuffled in the deck. It is needless to say that I do not know which cards were selected, or that I have no idea where they are. However, we shall look at those near the top and bottom to see if any are in that position." (Turn deck over and show two or three of the bottom cards, turn deck back and take off top three in right hand, showing faces; then as replacing, push over next card with the left thumb, so that left little finger may be inserted under it, and shift all four to the bottom. This will leave A.'s two cards at top and bottom.) "Were any of the selected cards among those I have just shown? No? Well, I am about to perform what under ordinary circumstances would be a very difficult feat indeed, but with this trained and perfectly educated deck, becomes ridiculously simple and easy. It is to cause the selected cards to appear at the top and bottom, in any order that you may desire." (To A.) "If you will tell me, sir, what cards you drew, I shall call upon them to appear instantly. You say they are the Seven of Diamonds and the Jack of Spades? Well, now, Seven and Jack, come!" (Hold deck in left hand, click with little finger, show bottom card, take off top and show with right hand, push next card over side when replacing and shift two to bottom. This leaves B.'s cards at top and bottom.) "You see how willingly the cards obey me. Now, sir (to B.), let me know the cards you selected and we shall see if they are as active." (When names are given, produce as before. Now execute blind shuffle again, running three extra cards on top. Again show several at bottom, then show top three, and this time push over two cards with left thumb when replacing top cards, and shift five to bottom. This leaves B.'s cards in position.) "We have still another pair to find, and though they seem excessively modest in keeping away from the top and bottom, I have no doubt they will be in evidence when called upon. What two did you draw, sir?" (to C. When names are given show as before, then shift two cards to bottom, leaving D.'s at top and bottom. Now affect to have forgotten about D.'s cards, and drop the deck on the table as though the trick were terminated. When reminded by the company that D.'s cards were not produced, show some slight embarrassment.) "Yes, that is true. I had forgotten that all were not produced, and as the deck has been out of my possession, I cannot exact the same obedience from them. However, if you will tell me the names of the last two cards, I shall try to find them myself." (When names are given, seize deck with right hand, toss it a yard or so straight upward, retaining top and bottom cards in hand by friction, thrust hand among descending pack and apparently find the last two in the act.)

The Three Aces. — In Effect: The Ace of Diamonds, Ace of Clubs and Ace of Spades are shown to the company and laid face down on the table. Then one is picked up and inserted in the middle of the deck, another is placed on the bottom, and the third is placed on the top. A single true cut is now made and the three Aces are found together.

Sleight: Prearrangement.

Execution: Secretly place the Ace of Diamonds on top of the deck. Arrange the other three Aces in the left hand, fanwise, face up, the Ace of Hearts below the other two, and showing in the middle. The figure of the heart is inverted and shows at the angle made by the other cards, so that the part seen is diamond-shaped. The corner of the Ace on the left of the fan just covers the small heart figure of the index, but fully exposes the small letter "A." (See Fig. 101.) This arrangement can be made in a moment. The appearance is most innocent and surprisingly deceptive.

Turn the faces to the company, and then lay the three cards face down on the table, still in the same fan position, and with the same hand. Now take up the deck, and, if desired, execute a blind shuffle, retaining top Ace. Hold deck in left hand, pick up the top card of the fan, which is the Ace of Hearts, and insert it in middle of deck. Pick up next Ace, carelessly showing it, and place it on bottom. Show third card as it is placed on top. Lay the deck on the table and request spectator to cut; and as the three Aces, i. e., the two black Aces and Ace of Diamonds, were on top and bottom of deck, all will be found together.

Fig. 101

The Card and Hat. — In Effect: A borrowed hat is placed upon the table. A card is now freely selected and given to a second spectator to hold. Attention is now drawn to the hat, which is shown to be empty, and it is again placed on the table, but crown up. The selected card is then restored to the deck by the spectator, who is permitted to take the deck in his own hands. The performer now exercises very remarkable powers by first determining the name of the selected card, and then causing it to wing an invisible flight from the deck to a position beneath the hat on the table, where it is found by a spectator.

Sleights: Top Change and Palm.

Execution: Borrow the hat first and place it rim up on the table. Have a card selected by spectator on the left. Take it from him with the right hand, and when turning to spectator on the right, make "Top Change," and request second spectator to hold the card between his two palms; which will prevent him from looking at it. Now palm top card in right hand and give deck to first spectator to hold. Step towards table, getting glimpse of palmed card, and pick up the hat with right hand, fingers well inside, thumb across rim, calling attention to the fact that it is empty, and showing the inside. Now turn the rim down and place the hat again upon the table, working the palmed card up along the inside with the fingers, and releasing it as the hat is laid down. Care must be taken to leave no crimp in the card.

Now take deck from first spectator, request second spectator to hold it in the hand that happens to be uppermost. Then take the card from his other hand and insert it in the deck, and have spectator shuffle thoroughly.

As the action is now complete, make by-play of determining the name of the drawn card, by tracing the very faint impression that it left on the palm of spectator who held it; and cause it to speed from the deck, under the hat, visibly if desired, expressing surprise that no one sees it going, and have spectator raise the hat to prove there is no hocus-pocus.

A CATALOG OF SELECTED
DOVER BOOKS
IN ALL FIELDS OF INTEREST

A CATALOG OF SELECTED DOVER
BOOKS IN ALL FIELDS OF INTEREST

CONCERNING THE SPIRITUAL IN ART, Wassily Kandinsky. Pioneering work by father of abstract art. Thoughts on color theory, nature of art. Analysis of earlier masters. 12 illustrations. 80pp. of text. 5⅜ × 8½.   23411-8 Pa. $3.95

ANIMALS: 1,419 Copyright-Free Illustrations of Mammals, Birds, Fish, Insects, etc., Jim Harter (ed.). Clear wood engravings present, in extremely lifelike poses, over 1,000 species of animals. One of the most extensive pictorial sourcebooks of its kind. Captions. Index. 284pp. 9 × 12.   23766-4 Pa. $11.95

CELTIC ART: The Methods of Construction, George Bain. Simple geometric techniques for making Celtic interlacements, spirals, Kells-type initials, animals, humans, etc. Over 500 illustrations. 160pp. 9 × 12. (USO)   22923-8 Pa. $8.95

AN ATLAS OF ANATOMY FOR ARTISTS, Fritz Schider. Most thorough reference work on art anatomy in the world. Hundreds of illustrations, including selections from works by Vesalius, Leonardo, Goya, Ingres, Michelangelo, others. 593 illustrations. 192pp. 7⅛ × 10¼.   20241-0 Pa. $8.95

CELTIC HAND STROKE-BY-STROKE (Irish Half-Uncial from "The Book of Kells"): An Arthur Baker Calligraphy Manual, Arthur Baker. Complete guide to creating each letter of the alphabet in distinctive Celtic manner. Covers hand position, strokes, pens, inks, paper, more. Illustrated. 48pp. 8¼ × 11.
24336-2 Pa. $3.95

EASY ORIGAMI, John Montroll. Charming collection of 32 projects (hat, cup, pelican, piano, swan, many more) specially designed for the novice origami hobbyist. Clearly illustrated easy-to-follow instructions insure that even beginning papercrafters will achieve successful results. 48pp. 8¼ × 11.   27298-2 Pa. $2.95

THE COMPLETE BOOK OF BIRDHOUSE CONSTRUCTION FOR WOOD-WORKERS, Scott D. Campbell. Detailed instructions, illustrations, tables. Also data on bird habitat and instinct patterns. Bibliography. 3 tables. 63 illustrations in 15 figures. 48pp. 5¼ × 8½.   24407-5 Pa. $1.95

BLOOMINGDALE'S ILLUSTRATED 1886 CATALOG: Fashions, Dry Goods and Housewares, Bloomingdale Brothers. Famed merchants' extremely rare catalog depicting about 1,700 products: clothing, housewares, firearms, dry goods, jewelry, more. Invaluable for dating, identifying vintage items. Also, copyright-free graphics for artists, designers. Co-published with Henry Ford Museum & Green-field Village. 160pp. 8¼ × 11.   25780-0 Pa. $9.95

HISTORIC COSTUME IN PICTURES, Braun & Schneider. Over 1,450 costumed figures in clearly detailed engravings—from dawn of civilization to end of 19th century. Captions. Many folk costumes. 256pp. 8⅜ × 11¾.   23150-X Pa. $10.95

CATALOG OF DOVER BOOKS

STICKLEY CRAFTSMAN FURNITURE CATALOGS, Gustav Stickley and L. & J. G. Stickley. Beautiful, functional furniture in two authentic catalogs from 1910. 594 illustrations, including 277 photos, show settles, rockers, armchairs, reclining chairs, bookcases, desks, tables. 183pp. 6½ × 9¼. 23838-5 Pa. $8.95

AMERICAN LOCOMOTIVES IN HISTORIC PHOTOGRAPHS: 1858 to 1949, Ron Ziel (ed.). A rare collection of 126 meticulously detailed official photographs, called "builder portraits," of American locomotives that majestically chronicle the rise of steam locomotive power in America. Introduction. Detailed captions. xi + 129pp. 9 × 12. 27393-8 Pa. $12.95

AMERICA'S LIGHTHOUSES: An Illustrated History, Francis Ross Holland, Jr. Delightfully written, profusely illustrated fact-filled survey of over 200 American lighthouses since 1716. History, anecdotes, technological advances, more. 240pp. 8 × 10¾. 25576-X Pa. $11.95

TOWARDS A NEW ARCHITECTURE, Le Corbusier. Pioneering manifesto by founder of "International School." Technical and aesthetic theories, views of industry, economics, relation of form to function, "mass-production split" and much more. Profusely illustrated. 320pp. 6⅛ × 9¼. (USO) 25023-7 Pa. $8.95

HOW THE OTHER HALF LIVES, Jacob Riis. Famous journalistic record, exposing poverty and degradation of New York slums around 1900, by major social reformer. 100 striking and influential photographs. 233pp. 10 × 7⅞.
22012-5 Pa $10.95

FRUIT KEY AND TWIG KEY TO TREES AND SHRUBS, William M. Harlow. One of the handiest and most widely used identification aids. Fruit key covers 120 deciduous and evergreen species; twig key 160 deciduous species. Easily used. Over 300 photographs. 126pp. 5⅜ × 8½. 20511-8 Pa. $3.95

COMMON BIRD SONGS, Dr. Donald J. Borror. Songs of 60 most common U.S. birds: robins, sparrows, cardinals, bluejays, finches, more—arranged in order of increasing complexity. Up to 9 variations of songs of each species.
Cassette and manual 99911-4 $8.95

ORCHIDS AS HOUSE PLANTS, Rebecca Tyson Northen. Grow cattleyas and many other kinds of orchids—in a window, in a case, or under artificial light. 63 illustrations. 148pp. 5⅜ × 8½. 23261-1 Pa. $3.95

MONSTER MAZES, Dave Phillips. Masterful mazes at four levels of difficulty. Avoid deadly perils and evil creatures to find magical treasures. Solutions for all 32 exciting illustrated puzzles. 48pp. 8¼ × 11. 26005-4 Pa. $2.95

MOZART'S DON GIOVANNI (DOVER OPERA LIBRETTO SERIES), Wolfgang Amadeus Mozart. Introduced and translated by Ellen H. Bleiler. Standard Italian libretto, with complete English translation. Convenient and thoroughly portable—an ideal companion for reading along with a recording or the performance itself. Introduction. List of characters. Plot summary. 121pp. 5¼ × 8½.
24944-1 Pa. $2.95

TECHNICAL MANUAL AND DICTIONARY OF CLASSICAL BALLET, Gail Grant. Defines, explains, comments on steps, movements, poses and concepts. 15-page pictorial section. Basic book for student, viewer. 127pp. 5⅜ × 8½.
21843-0 Pa. $3.95

BRASS INSTRUMENTS: Their History and Development, Anthony Baines. Authoritative, updated survey of the evolution of trumpets, trombones, bugles, cornets, French horns, tubas and other brass wind instruments. Over 140 illustrations and 48 music examples. Corrected and updated by author. New preface. Bibliography. 320pp. 5⅜ × 8½. 27574-4 Pa. $9.95

HOLLYWOOD GLAMOR PORTRAITS, John Kobal (ed.). 145 photos from 1926–49. Harlow, Gable, Bogart, Bacall; 94 stars in all. Full background on photographers, technical aspects. 160pp. 8⅜ × 11¼. 23352-9 Pa. $9.95

MAX AND MORITZ, Wilhelm Busch. Great humor classic in both German and English. Also 10 other works: "Cat and Mouse," "Plisch and Plumm," etc. 216pp. 5⅜ × 8½. 20181-3 Pa. $5.95

THE RAVEN AND OTHER FAVORITE POEMS, Edgar Allan Poe. Over 40 of the author's most memorable poems: "The Bells," "Ulalume," "Israfel," "To Helen," "The Conqueror Worm," "Eldorado," "Annabel Lee," many more. Alphabetic lists of titles and first lines. 64pp. 5³⁄₁₆ × 8¼. 26685-0 Pa. $1.00

SEVEN SCIENCE FICTION NOVELS, H. G. Wells. The standard collection of the great novels. Complete, unabridged. First Men in the Moon, Island of Dr. Moreau, War of the Worlds, Food of the Gods, Invisible Man, Time Machine, In the Days of the Comet. Total of 1,015pp. 5⅜ × 8½. (USO) 20264-X Clothbd. $29.95

AMULETS AND SUPERSTITIONS, E. A. Wallis Budge. Comprehensive discourse on origin, powers of amulets in many ancient cultures: Arab, Persian, Babylonian, Assyrian, Egyptian, Gnostic, Hebrew, Phoenician, Syriac, etc. Covers cross, swastika, crucifix, seals, rings, stones, etc. 584pp. 5⅜ × 8½. 23573-4 Pa. $12.95

RUSSIAN STORIES/PYCCKNE PACCKA3bl: A Dual-Language Book, edited by Gleb Struve. Twelve tales by such masters as Chekhov, Tolstoy, Dostoevsky, Pushkin, others. Excellent word-for-word English translations on facing pages, plus teaching and study aids, Russian/English vocabulary, biographical/critical introductions, more. 416pp. 5⅜ × 8½. 26244-8 Pa. $8.95

PHILADELPHIA THEN AND NOW: 60 Sites Photographed in the Past and Present, Kenneth Finkel and Susan Oyama. Rare photographs of City Hall, Logan Square, Independence Hall, Betsy Ross House, other landmarks juxtaposed with contemporary views. Captures changing face of historic city. Introduction. Captions. 128pp. 8¼ × 11. 25790-8 Pa. $9.95

AIA ARCHITECTURAL GUIDE TO NASSAU AND SUFFOLK COUNTIES, LONG ISLAND, The American Institute of Architects, Long Island Chapter, and the Society for the Preservation of Long Island Antiquities. Comprehensive, well-researched and generously illustrated volume brings to life over three centuries of Long Island's great architectural heritage. More than 240 photographs with authoritative, extensively detailed captions. 176pp. 8¼ × 11. 26946-9 Pa. $14.95

NORTH AMERICAN INDIAN LIFE: Customs and Traditions of 23 Tribes, Elsie Clews Parsons (ed.). 27 fictionalized essays by noted anthropologists examine religion, customs, government, additional facets of life among the Winnebago, Crow, Zuni, Eskimo, other tribes. 480pp. 6⅛ × 9¼. 27377-6 Pa. $10.95

FRANK LLOYD WRIGHT'S HOLLYHOCK HOUSE, Donald Hoffmann. Lavishly illustrated, carefully documented study of one of Wright's most controversial residential designs. Over 120 photographs, floor plans, elevations, etc. Detailed perceptive text by noted Wright scholar. Index. 128pp. 9¼ × 10¾.
27133-1 Pa. $11.95

THE MALE AND FEMALE FIGURE IN MOTION: 60 Classic Photographic Sequences, Eadweard Muybridge. 60 true-action photographs of men and women walking, running, climbing, bending, turning, etc., reproduced from rare 19th-century masterpiece. vi + 121pp. 9 × 12.
24745-7 Pa. $10.95

1001 QUESTIONS ANSWERED ABOUT THE SEASHORE, N. J. Berrill and Jacquelyn Berrill. Queries answered about dolphins, sea snails, sponges, starfish, fishes, shore birds, many others. Covers appearance, breeding, growth, feeding, much more. 305pp. 5¼ × 8¼.
23366-9 Pa. $7.95

GUIDE TO OWL WATCHING IN NORTH AMERICA, Donald S. Heintzelman. Superb guide offers complete data and descriptions of 19 species: barn owl, screech owl, snowy owl, many more. Expert coverage of owl-watching equipment, conservation, migrations and invasions, etc. Guide to observing sites. 84 illustrations. xiii + 193pp. 5⅜ × 8½.
27344-X Pa. $7.95

MEDICINAL AND OTHER USES OF NORTH AMERICAN PLANTS: A Historical Survey with Special Reference to the Eastern Indian Tribes, Charlotte Erichsen-Brown. Chronological historical citations document 500 years of usage of plants, trees, shrubs native to eastern Canada, northeastern U.S. Also complete identifying information. 343 illustrations. 544pp. 6½ × 9¼.
25951-X Pa. $12.95

STORYBOOK MAZES, Dave Phillips. 23 stories and mazes on two-page spreads: Wizard of Oz, Treasure Island, Robin Hood, etc. Solutions. 64pp. 8¼ × 11.
23628-5 Pa. $2.95

NEGRO FOLK MUSIC, U.S.A., Harold Courlander. Noted folklorist's scholarly yet readable analysis of rich and varied musical tradition. Includes authentic versions of over 40 folk songs. Valuable bibliography and discography. xi + 324pp. 5⅜ × 8½.
27350-4 Pa. $7.95

MOVIE-STAR PORTRAITS OF THE FORTIES, John Kobal (ed.). 163 glamor, studio photos of 106 stars of the 1940s: Rita Hayworth, Ava Gardner, Marlon Brando, Clark Gable, many more. 176pp. 8⅜ × 11¼.
23546-7 Pa. $10.95

BENCHLEY LOST AND FOUND, Robert Benchley. Finest humor from early 30s, about pet peeves, child psychologists, post office and others. Mostly unavailable elsewhere. 73 illustrations by Peter Arno and others. 183pp. 5⅜ × 8½.
22410-4 Pa. $5.95

YEKL and THE IMPORTED BRIDEGROOM AND OTHER STORIES OF YIDDISH NEW YORK, Abraham Cahan. Film Hester Street based on Yekl (1896). Novel, other stories among first about Jewish immigrants on N.Y.'s East Side. 240pp. 5⅜ × 8½.
22427-9 Pa. $5.95

SELECTED POEMS, Walt Whitman. Generous sampling from *Leaves of Grass.* Twenty-four poems include "I Hear America Singing," "Song of the Open Road," "I Sing the Body Electric," "When Lilacs Last in the Dooryard Bloom'd," "O Captain! My Captain!"—all reprinted from an authoritative edition. Lists of titles and first lines. 128pp. 5³⁄₁₆ × 8¼.
26878-0 Pa. $1.00

THE BEST TALES OF HOFFMANN, E. T. A. Hoffmann. 10 of Hoffmann's most important stories: "Nutcracker and the King of Mice," "The Golden Flowerpot," etc. 458pp. 5⅜ × 8½. 21793-0 Pa. $8.95

FROM FETISH TO GOD IN ANCIENT EGYPT, E. A. Wallis Budge. Rich detailed survey of Egyptian conception of "God" and gods, magic, cult of animals, Osiris, more. Also, superb English translations of hymns and legends. 240 illustrations. 545pp. 5⅜ × 8½. 25803-3 Pa. $11.95

FRENCH STORIES/CONTES FRANÇAIS: A Dual-Language Book, Wallace Fowlie. Ten stories by French masters, Voltaire to Camus: "Micromegas" by Voltaire; "The Atheist's Mass" by Balzac; "Minuet" by de Maupassant; "The Guest" by Camus, six more. Excellent English translations on facing pages. Also French-English vocabulary list, exercises, more. 352pp. 5⅜ × 8½. 26443-2 Pa. $8.95

CHICAGO AT THE TURN OF THE CENTURY IN PHOTOGRAPHS: 122 Historic Views from the Collections of the Chicago Historical Society, Larry A. Viskochil. Rare large-format prints offer detailed views of City Hall, State Street, the Loop, Hull House, Union Station, many other landmarks, circa 1904–1913. Introduction. Captions. Maps. 144pp. 9⅜ × 12¼. 24656-6 Pa. $12.95

OLD BROOKLYN IN EARLY PHOTOGRAPHS, 1865–1929, William Lee Younger. Luna Park, Gravesend race track, construction of Grand Army Plaza, moving of Hotel Brighton, etc. 157 previously unpublished photographs. 165pp. 8⅞ × 11¾. 23587-4 Pa. $12.95

THE MYTHS OF THE NORTH AMERICAN INDIANS, Lewis Spence. Rich anthology of the myths and legends of the Algonquins, Iroquois, Pawnees and Sioux, prefaced by an extensive historical and ethnological commentary. 36 illustrations. 480pp. 5⅜ × 8½. 25967-6 Pa. $8.95

AN ENCYCLOPEDIA OF BATTLES: Accounts of Over 1,560 Battles from 1479 B.C. to the Present, David Eggenberger. Essential details of every major battle in recorded history from the first battle of Megiddo in 1479 B.C. to Grenada in 1984. List of Battle Maps. New Appendix covering the years 1967–1984. Index. 99 illustrations. 544pp. 6½ × 9¼. 24913-1 Pa. $14.95

SAILING ALONE AROUND THE WORLD, Captain Joshua Slocum. First man to sail around the world, alone, in small boat. One of great feats of seamanship told in delightful manner. 67 illustrations. 294pp. 5⅜ × 8½. 20326-3 Pa. $5.95

ANARCHISM AND OTHER ESSAYS, Emma Goldman. Powerful, penetrating, prophetic essays on direct action, role of minorities, prison reform, puritan hypocrisy, violence, etc. 271pp. 5⅜ × 8½. 22484-8 Pa. $5.95

MYTHS OF THE HINDUS AND BUDDHISTS, Ananda K. Coomaraswamy and Sister Nivedita. Great stories of the epics; deeds of Krishna, Shiva, taken from puranas, Vedas, folk tales; etc. 32 illustrations. 400pp. 5⅜ × 8½. 21759-0 Pa. $9.95

BEYOND PSYCHOLOGY, Otto Rank. Fear of death, desire of immortality, nature of sexuality, social organization, creativity, according to Rankian system. 291pp. 5⅜ × 8½. 20485-5 Pa. $7.95

A THEOLOGICO-POLITICAL TREATISE, Benedict Spinoza. Also contains unfinished Political Treatise. Great classic on religious liberty, theory of government on common consent. R. Elwes translation. Total of 421pp. 5⅜ × 8½. 20249-6 Pa. $7.95

MY BONDAGE AND MY FREEDOM, Frederick Douglass. Born a slave, Douglass became outspoken force in antislavery movement. The best of Douglass' autobiographies. Graphic description of slave life. 464pp. 5⅜ × 8½.　22457-0 Pa. $8.95

FOLLOWING THE EQUATOR: A Journey Around the World, Mark Twain. Fascinating humorous account of 1897 voyage to Hawaii, Australia, India, New Zealand, etc. Ironic, bemused reports on peoples, customs, climate, flora and fauna, politics, much more. 197 illustrations. 720pp. 5⅜ × 8½.　26113-1 Pa. $15.95

THE PEOPLE CALLED SHAKERS, Edward D. Andrews. Definitive study of Shakers: origins, beliefs, practices, dances, social organization, furniture and crafts, etc. 33 illustrations. 351pp. 5⅜ × 8½.　21081-2 Pa. $7.95

THE MYTHS OF GREECE AND ROME, H. A. Guerber. A classic of mythology, generously illustrated, long prized for its simple, graphic, accurate retelling of the principal myths of Greece and Rome, and for its commentary on their origins and significance. With 64 illustrations by Michelangelo, Raphael, Titian, Rubens, Canova, Bernini and others. 480pp. 5⅜ × 8½.　27584-1 Pa. $9.95

PSYCHOLOGY OF MUSIC, Carl E. Seashore. Classic work discusses music as a medium from psychological viewpoint. Clear treatment of physical acoustics, auditory apparatus, sound perception, development of musical skills, nature of musical feeling, host of other topics. 88 figures. 408pp. 5⅜ × 8½.　21851-1 Pa. $9.95

THE PHILOSOPHY OF HISTORY, Georg W. Hegel. Great classic of Western thought develops concept that history is not chance but rational process, the evolution of freedom. 457pp. 5⅜ × 8½.　20112-0 Pa. $8.95

THE BOOK OF TEA, Kakuzo Okakura. Minor classic of the Orient: entertaining, charming explanation, interpretation of traditional Japanese culture in terms of tea ceremony. 94pp. 5⅜ × 8½.　20070-1 Pa. $2.95

LIFE IN ANCIENT EGYPT, Adolf Erman. Fullest, most thorough, detailed older account with much not in more recent books, domestic life, religion, magic, medicine, commerce, much more. Many illustrations reproduce tomb paintings, carvings, hieroglyphs, etc. 597pp. 5⅜ × 8½.　22632-8 Pa. $9.95

SUNDIALS, Their Theory and Construction, Albert Waugh. Far and away the best, most thorough coverage of ideas, mathematics concerned, types, construction, adjusting anywhere. Simple, nontechnical treatment allows even children to build several of these dials. Over 100 illustrations. 230pp. 5⅜ × 8½.　22947-5 Pa. $5.95

DYNAMICS OF FLUIDS IN POROUS MEDIA, Jacob Bear. For advanced students of ground water hydrology, soil mechanics and physics, drainage and irrigation engineering, and more. 335 illustrations. Exercises, with answers. 784pp. 6⅛ × 9¼.　65675-6 Pa. $19.95

SONGS OF EXPERIENCE: Facsimile Reproduction with 26 Plates in Full Color, William Blake. 26 full-color plates from a rare 1826 edition. Includes "The Tyger," "London," "Holy Thursday," and other poems. Printed text of poems. 48pp. 5¼ × 7.　24636-1 Pa. $3.95

OLD-TIME VIGNETTES IN FULL COLOR, Carol Belanger Grafton (ed.). Over 390 charming, often sentimental illustrations, selected from archives of Victorian graphics—pretty women posing, children playing, food, flowers, kittens and puppies, smiling cherubs, birds and butterflies, much more. All copyright-free. 48pp. 9¼ × 12¼.　27269-9 Pa. $5.95

PERSPECTIVE FOR ARTISTS, Rex Vicat Cole. Depth, perspective of sky and sea, shadows, much more, not usually covered. 391 diagrams, 81 reproductions of drawings and paintings. 279pp. 5⅜ × 8½. 22487-2 Pa. $6.95

DRAWING THE LIVING FIGURE, Joseph Sheppard. Innovative approach to artistic anatomy focuses on specifics of surface anatomy, rather than muscles and bones. Over 170 drawings of live models in front, back and side views, and in widely varying poses. Accompanying diagrams. 177 illustrations. Introduction. Index. 144pp. 8⅜ × 11¼. 26723-7 Pa. $7.95

GOTHIC AND OLD ENGLISH ALPHABETS: 100 Complete Fonts, Dan X. Solo. Add power, elegance to posters, signs, other graphics with 100 stunning copyright-free alphabets: Blackstone, Dolbey, Germania, 97 more—including many lower-case, numerals, punctuation marks. 104pp. 8⅛ × 11. 24695-7 Pa. $7.95

HOW TO DO BEADWORK, Mary White. Fundamental book on craft from simple projects to five-bead chains and woven works. 106 illustrations. 142pp. 5⅜ × 8. 20697-1 Pa. $4.95

THE BOOK OF WOOD CARVING, Charles Marshall Sayers. Finest book for beginners discusses fundamentals and offers 34 designs. "Absolutely first rate . . . well thought out and well executed."—E. J. Tangerman. 118pp. 7¾ × 10⅝. 23654-4 Pa. $5.95

ILLUSTRATED CATALOG OF CIVIL WAR MILITARY GOODS: Union Army Weapons, Insignia, Uniform Accessories, and Other Equipment, Schuyler, Hartley, and Graham. Rare, profusely illustrated 1846 catalog includes Union Army uniform and dress regulations, arms and ammunition, coats, insignia, flags, swords, rifles, etc. 226 illustrations. 160pp. 9 × 12. 24939-5 Pa. $10.95

WOMEN'S FASHIONS OF THE EARLY 1900s: An Unabridged Republication of "New York Fashions, 1909," National Cloak & Suit Co. Rare catalog of mail-order fashions documents women's and children's clothing styles shortly after the turn of the century. Captions offer full descriptions, prices. Invaluable resource for fashion, costume historians. Approximately 725 illustrations. 128pp. 8⅜ × 11¼. 27276-1 Pa. $10.95

THE 1912 AND 1915 GUSTAV STICKLEY FURNITURE CATALOGS, Gustav Stickley. With over 200 detailed illustrations and descriptions, these two catalogs are essential reading and reference materials and identification guides for Stickley furniture. Captions cite materials, dimensions and prices. 112pp. 6½ × 9¼. 26676-1 Pa. $9.95

EARLY AMERICAN LOCOMOTIVES, John H. White, Jr. Finest locomotive engravings from early 19th century: historical (1804–74), main-line (after 1870), special, foreign, etc. 147 plates. 142pp. 11⅜ × 8¼. 22772-3 Pa. $8.95

THE TALL SHIPS OF TODAY IN PHOTOGRAPHS, Frank O. Braynard. Lavishly illustrated tribute to nearly 100 majestic contemporary sailing vessels: Amerigo Vespucci, Clearwater, Constitution, Eagle, Mayflower, Sea Cloud, Victory, many more. Authoritative captions provide statistics, background on each ship. 190 black-and-white photographs and illustrations. Introduction. 128pp. 8⅞ × 11¾. 27163-3 Pa. $12.95

EARLY NINETEENTH-CENTURY CRAFTS AND TRADES, Peter Stockham (ed.). Extremely rare 1807 volume describes to youngsters the crafts and trades of the day: brickmaker, weaver, dressmaker, bookbinder, ropemaker, saddler, many more. Quaint prose, charming illustrations for each craft. 20 black-and-white line illustrations. 192pp. 4⅝ × 6. 27293-1 Pa. $4.95

VICTORIAN FASHIONS AND COSTUMES FROM HARPER'S BAZAR, 1867–1898, Stella Blum (ed.). Day costumes, evening wear, sports clothes, shoes, hats, other accessories in over 1,000 detailed engravings. 320pp. 9⅜ × 12¼.
22990-4 Pa. $13.95

GUSTAV STICKLEY, THE CRAFTSMAN, Mary Ann Smith. Superb study surveys broad scope of Stickley's achievement, especially in architecture. Design philosophy, rise and fall of the Craftsman empire, descriptions and floor plans for many Craftsman houses, more. 86 black-and-white halftones. 31 line illustrations. Introduction. 208pp. 6½ × 9¼. 27210-9 Pa. $9.95

THE LONG ISLAND RAIL ROAD IN EARLY PHOTOGRAPHS, Ron Ziel. Over 220 rare photos, informative text document origin (1844) and development of rail service on Long Island. Vintage views of early trains, locomotives, stations, passengers, crews, much more. Captions. 8⅞ × 11¾. 26301-0 Pa. $13.95

THE BOOK OF OLD SHIPS: From Egyptian Galleys to Clipper Ships, Henry B. Culver. Superb, authoritative history of sailing vessels, with 80 magnificent line illustrations. Galley, bark, caravel, longship, whaler, many more. Detailed, informative text on each vessel by noted naval historian. Introduction. 256pp. 5⅜ × 8½. 27332-6 Pa. $6.95

TEN BOOKS ON ARCHITECTURE, Vitruvius. The most important book ever written on architecture. Early Roman aesthetics, technology, classical orders, site selection, all other aspects. Morgan translation. 331pp. 5⅜ × 8½. 20645-9 Pa. $8.95

THE HUMAN FIGURE IN MOTION, Eadweard Muybridge. More than 4,500 stopped-action photos, in action series, showing undraped men, women, children jumping, lying down, throwing, sitting, wrestling, carrying, etc. 390pp. 7⅞ × 10⅝.
20204-6 Clothbd. $24.95

TREES OF THE EASTERN AND CENTRAL UNITED STATES AND CANADA, William M. Harlow. Best one-volume guide to 140 trees. Full descriptions, woodlore, range, etc. Over 600 illustrations. Handy size. 288pp. 4½ × 6⅜.
20395-6 Pa. $5.95

SONGS OF WESTERN BIRDS, Dr. Donald J. Borror. Complete song and call repertoire of 60 western species, including flycatchers, juncoes, cactus wrens, many more—includes fully illustrated booklet. Cassette and manual 99913-0 $8.95

GROWING AND USING HERBS AND SPICES, Milo Miloradovich. Versatile handbook provides all the information needed for cultivation and use of all the herbs and spices available in North America. 4 illustrations. Index. Glossary. 236pp. 5⅜ × 8½. 25058-X Pa. $5.95

BIG BOOK OF MAZES AND LABYRINTHS, Walter Shepherd. 50 mazes and labyrinths in all—classical, solid, ripple, and more—in one great volume. Perfect inexpensive puzzler for clever youngsters. Full solutions. 112pp. 8⅛ × 11.
22951-3 Pa. $3.95

PIANO TUNING, J. Cree Fischer. Clearest, best book for beginner, amateur. Simple repairs, raising dropped notes, tuning by easy method of flattened fifths. No previous skills needed. 4 illustrations. 201pp. 5⅜ × 8½.   23267-0 Pa. $5.95

A SOURCE BOOK IN THEATRICAL HISTORY, A. M. Nagler. Contemporary observers on acting, directing, make-up, costuming, stage props, machinery, scene design, from Ancient Greece to Chekhov. 611pp. 5⅜ × 8½.   20515-0 Pa. $11.95

THE COMPLETE NONSENSE OF EDWARD LEAR, Edward Lear. All nonsense limericks, zany alphabets, Owl and Pussycat, songs, nonsense botany, etc., illustrated by Lear. Total of 320pp. 5⅜ × 8½. (USO)   20167-8 Pa. $5.95

VICTORIAN PARLOUR POETRY: An Annotated Anthology, Michael R. Turner. 117 gems by Longfellow, Tennyson, Browning, many lesser-known poets. "The Village Blacksmith," "Curfew Must Not Ring Tonight," "Only a Baby Small," dozens more, often difficult to find elsewhere. Index of poets, titles, first lines. xxiii + 325pp. 5⅜ × 8¼.   27044-0 Pa. $8.95

DUBLINERS, James Joyce. Fifteen stories offer vivid, tightly focused observations of the lives of Dublin's poorer classes. At least one, "The Dead," is considered a masterpiece. Reprinted complete and unabridged from standard edition. 160pp. 5³⁄₁₆ × 8¼.   26870-5 Pa. $1.00

THE HAUNTED MONASTERY and THE CHINESE MAZE MURDERS, Robert van Gulik. Two full novels by van Gulik, set in 7th-century China, continue adventures of Judge Dee and his companions. An evil Taoist monastery, seemingly supernatural events; overgrown topiary maze hides strange crimes. 27 illustrations. 328pp. 5⅜ × 8½.   23502-5 Pa. $7.95

THE BOOK OF THE SACRED MAGIC OF ABRAMELIN THE MAGE, translated by S. MacGregor Mathers. Medieval manuscript of ceremonial magic. Basic document in Aleister Crowley, Golden Dawn groups. 268pp. 5⅜ × 8½.
                          23211-5 Pa. $7.95

NEW RUSSIAN-ENGLISH AND ENGLISH-RUSSIAN DICTIONARY, M. A. O'Brien. This is a remarkably handy Russian dictionary, containing a surprising amount of information, including over 70,000 entries. 366pp. 4½ × 6⅛.
                          20208-9 Pa. $8.95

HISTORIC HOMES OF THE AMERICAN PRESIDENTS, Second, Revised Edition, Irvin Haas. A traveler's guide to American Presidential homes, most open to the public, depicting and describing homes occupied by every American President from George Washington to George Bush. With visiting hours, admission charges, travel routes. 175 photographs. Index. 160pp. 8¼ × 11. 26751-2 Pa. $10.95

NEW YORK IN THE FORTIES, Andreas Feininger. 162 brilliant photographs by the well-known photographer, formerly with *Life* magazine. Commuters, shoppers, Times Square at night, much else from city at its peak. Captions by John von Hartz. 181pp. 9¼ × 10¾.   23585-8 Pa. $12.95

INDIAN SIGN LANGUAGE, William Tomkins. Over 525 signs developed by Sioux and other tribes. Written instructions and diagrams. Also 290 pictographs. 111pp. 6⅛ × 9¼.   22029-X Pa. $3.50

ANATOMY: A Complete Guide for Artists, Joseph Sheppard. A master of figure drawing shows artists how to render human anatomy convincingly. Over 460 illustrations. 224pp. 8⅜ × 11¼. 27279-6 Pa. $9.95

MEDIEVAL CALLIGRAPHY: Its History and Technique, Marc Drogin. Spirited history, comprehensive instruction manual covers 13 styles (ca. 4th century thru 15th). Excellent photographs; directions for duplicating medieval techniques with modern tools. 224pp. 8⅜ × 11¼. 26142-5 Pa. $11.95

DRIED FLOWERS: How to Prepare Them, Sarah Whitlock and Martha Rankin. Complete instructions on how to use silica gel, meal and borax, perlite aggregate, sand and borax, glycerine and water to create attractive permanent flower arrangements. 12 illustrations. 32pp. 5⅜ × 8½. 21802-3 Pa. $1.00

EASY-TO-MAKE BIRD FEEDERS FOR WOODWORKERS, Scott D. Campbell. Detailed, simple-to-use guide for designing, constructing, caring for and using feeders. Text, illustrations for 12 classic and contemporary designs. 96pp. 5⅜ × 8½. 25847-5 Pa. $2.95

OLD-TIME CRAFTS AND TRADES, Peter Stockham. An 1807 book created to teach children about crafts and trades open to them as future careers. It describes in detailed, nontechnical terms 24 different occupations, among them coachmaker, gardener, hairdresser, lacemaker, shoemaker, wheelwright, copper-plate printer, milliner, trunkmaker, merchant and brewer. Finely detailed engravings illustrate each occupation. 192pp. 4⅝ × 6. 27398-9 Pa. $4.95

THE HISTORY OF UNDERCLOTHES, C. Willett Cunnington and Phyllis Cunnington. Fascinating, well-documented survey covering six centuries of English undergarments, enhanced with over 100 illustrations: 12th-century laced-up bodice, footed long drawers (1795), 19th-century bustles, 19th-century corsets for men, Victorian "bust improvers," much more. 272pp. 5⅜ × 8¼. 27124-2 Pa. $9.95

ARTS AND CRAFTS FURNITURE: The Complete Brooks Catalog of 1912, Brooks Manufacturing Co. Photos and detailed descriptions of more than 150 now very collectible furniture designs from the Arts and Crafts movement depict davenports, settees, buffets, desks, tables, chairs, bedsteads, dressers and more, all built of solid, quarter-sawed oak. Invaluable for students and enthusiasts of antiques, Americana and the decorative arts. 80pp. 6½ × 9¼. 27471-3 Pa. $7.95

HOW WE INVENTED THE AIRPLANE: An Illustrated History, Orville Wright. Fascinating firsthand account covers early experiments, construction of planes and motors, first flights, much more. Introduction and commentary by Fred C. Kelly. 76 photographs. 96pp. 8¼ × 11. 25662-6 Pa. $7.95

THE ARTS OF THE SAILOR: Knotting, Splicing and Ropework, Hervey Garrett Smith. Indispensable shipboard reference covers tools, basic knots and useful hitches; handsewing and canvas work, more. Over 100 illustrations. Delightful reading for sea lovers. 256pp. 5⅜ × 8½. 26440-8 Pa. $7.95

FRANK LLOYD WRIGHT'S FALLINGWATER: The House and Its History, Second, Revised Edition, Donald Hoffmann. A total revision—both in text and illustrations—of the standard document on Fallingwater, the boldest, most personal architectural statement of Wright's mature years, updated with valuable new material from the recently opened Frank Lloyd Wright Archives. "Fascinating"—*The New York Times.* 116 illustrations. 128pp. 9¼ × 10¾. 27430-6 Pa. $10.95

PHOTOGRAPHIC SKETCHBOOK OF THE CIVIL WAR, Alexander Gardner. 100 photos taken on field during the Civil War. Famous shots of Manassas, Harper's Ferry, Lincoln, Richmond, slave pens, etc. 244pp. 10⅝ × 8¼.
22731-6 Pa. $9.95

FIVE ACRES AND INDEPENDENCE, Maurice G. Kains. Great back-to-the-land classic explains basics of self-sufficient farming. The one book to get. 95 illustrations. 397pp. 5⅜ × 8½.
20974-1 Pa. $6.95

SONGS OF EASTERN BIRDS, Dr. Donald J. Borror. Songs and calls of 60 species most common to eastern U.S.: warblers, woodpeckers, flycatchers, thrushes, larks, many more in high-quality recording.
Cassette and manual 99912-2 $8.95

A MODERN HERBAL, Margaret Grieve. Much the fullest, most exact, most useful compilation of herbal material. Gigantic alphabetical encyclopedia, from aconite to zedoary, gives botanical information, medical properties, folklore, economic uses, much else. Indispensable to serious reader. 161 illustrations. 888pp. 6½ × 9¼. 2-vol. set. (USO)
Vol. I: 22798-7 Pa. $9.95
Vol. II: 22799-5 Pa. $9.95

HIDDEN TREASURE MAZE BOOK, Dave Phillips. Solve 34 challenging mazes accompanied by heroic tales of adventure. Evil dragons, people-eating plants, bloodthirsty giants, many more dangerous adversaries lurk at every twist and turn. 34 mazes, stories, solutions. 48pp. 8¼ × 11.
24566-7 Pa. $2.95

LETTERS OF W. A. MOZART, Wolfgang A. Mozart. Remarkable letters show bawdy wit, humor, imagination, musical insights, contemporary musical world; includes some letters from Leopold Mozart. 276pp. 5⅜ × 8½.
22859-2 Pa. $6.95

BASIC PRINCIPLES OF CLASSICAL BALLET, Agrippina Vaganova. Great Russian theoretician, teacher explains methods for teaching classical ballet. 118 illustrations. 175pp. 5⅜ × 8½.
22036-2 Pa. $4.95

THE JUMPING FROG, Mark Twain. Revenge edition. The original story of The Celebrated Jumping Frog of Calaveras County, a hapless French translation, and Twain's hilarious "retranslation" from the French. 12 illustrations. 66pp. 5⅜ × 8½.
22686-7 Pa. $3.50

BEST REMEMBERED POEMS, Martin Gardner (ed.). The 126 poems in this superb collection of 19th- and 20th-century British and American verse range from Shelley's "To a Skylark" to the impassioned "Renascence" of Edna St. Vincent Millay and to Edward Lear's whimsical "The Owl and the Pussycat." 224pp. 5⅜ × 8½.
27165-X Pa. $4.95

COMPLETE SONNETS, William Shakespeare. Over 150 exquisite poems deal with love, friendship, the tyranny of time, beauty's evanescence, death and other themes in language of remarkable power, precision and beauty. Glossary of archaic terms. 80pp. 5³⁄₁₆ × 8¼.
26686-9 Pa. $1.00

BODIES IN A BOOKSHOP, R. T. Campbell. Challenging mystery of blackmail and murder with ingenious plot and superbly drawn characters. In the best tradition of British suspense fiction. 192pp. 5⅜ × 8½.
24720-1 Pa. $5.95

THE WIT AND HUMOR OF OSCAR WILDE, Alvin Redman (ed.). More than 1,000 ripostes, paradoxes, wisecracks: Work is the curse of the drinking classes; I can resist everything except temptation; etc. 258pp. 5⅜ × 8½. 20602-5 Pa. $4.95

SHAKESPEARE LEXICON AND QUOTATION DICTIONARY, Alexander Schmidt. Full definitions, locations, shades of meaning in every word in plays and poems. More than 50,000 exact quotations. 1,485pp. 6½ × 9¼. 2-vol. set.
Vol. 1: 22726-X Pa. $15.95
Vol. 2: 22727-8 Pa. $15.95

SELECTED POEMS, Emily Dickinson. Over 100 best-known, best-loved poems by one of America's foremost poets, reprinted from authoritative early editions. No comparable edition at this price. Index of first lines. 64pp. 5³/₁₆ × 8¼.
26466-1 Pa. $1.00

CELEBRATED CASES OF JUDGE DEE (DEE GOONG AN), translated by Robert van Gulik. Authentic 18th-century Chinese detective novel; Dee and associates solve three interlocked cases. Led to van Gulik's own stories with same characters. Extensive introduction. 9 illustrations. 237pp. 5⅜ × 8½.
23337-5 Pa. $5.95

THE MALLEUS MALEFICARUM OF KRAMER AND SPRENGER, translated by Montague Summers. Full text of most important witchhunter's "bible," used by both Catholics and Protestants. 278pp. 6⅝ × 10. 22802-9 Pa. $10.95

SPANISH STORIES/CUENTOS ESPAÑOLES: A Dual-Language Book, Angel Flores (ed.). Unique format offers 13 great stories in Spanish by Cervantes, Borges, others. Faithful English translations on facing pages. 352pp. 5⅜ × 8½.
25399-6 Pa. $8.95

THE CHICAGO WORLD'S FAIR OF 1893: A Photographic Record, Stanley Appelbaum (ed.). 128 rare photos show 200 buildings, Beaux-Arts architecture, Midway, original Ferris Wheel, Edison's kinetoscope, more. Architectural emphasis; full text. 116pp. 8¼ × 11. 23990-X Pa. $9.95

OLD QUEENS, N.Y., IN EARLY PHOTOGRAPHS, Vincent F. Seyfried and William Asadorian. Over 160 rare photographs of Maspeth, Jamaica, Jackson Heights, and other areas. Vintage views of DeWitt Clinton mansion, 1939 World's Fair and more. Captions. 192pp. 8⅞ × 11. 26358-4 Pa. $12.95

CAPTURED BY THE INDIANS: 15 Firsthand Accounts, 1750–1870, Frederick Drimmer. Astounding true historical accounts of grisly torture, bloody conflicts, relentless pursuits, miraculous escapes and more, by people who lived to tell the tale. 384pp. 5⅜ × 8½. 24901-8 Pa. $7.95

THE WORLD'S GREAT SPEECHES, Lewis Copeland and Lawrence W. Lamm (eds.). Vast collection of 278 speeches of Greeks to 1970. Powerful and effective models; unique look at history. 842pp. 5⅜ × 8½. 20468-5 Pa. $13.95

THE BOOK OF THE SWORD, Sir Richard F. Burton. Great Victorian scholar/adventurer's eloquent, erudite history of the "queen of weapons"—from prehistory to early Roman Empire. Evolution and development of early swords, variations (sabre, broadsword, cutlass, scimitar, etc.), much more. 336pp. 6⅛ × 9¼. 25434-8 Pa. $8.95

AUTOBIOGRAPHY: The Story of My Experiments with Truth, Mohandas K. Gandhi. Boyhood, legal studies, purification, the growth of the Satyagraha (nonviolent protest) movement. Critical, inspiring work of the man responsible for the freedom of India. 480pp. 5⅜ × 8½. (USO) 24593-4 Pa. $7.95

CELTIC MYTHS AND LEGENDS, T. W. Rolleston. Masterful retelling of Irish and Welsh stories and tales. Cuchulain, King Arthur, Deirdre, the Grail, many more. First paperback edition. 58 full-page illustrations. 512pp. 5⅜ × 8½.
26507-2 Pa. $9.95

THE PRINCIPLES OF PSYCHOLOGY, William James. Famous long course complete, unabridged. Stream of thought, time perception, memory, experimental methods; great work decades ahead of its time. 94 figures. 1,391pp. 5⅜×8½. 2-vol. set.
Vol. I: 20381-6 Pa. $12.95
Vol. II: 20382-4 Pa. $12.95

THE WORLD AS WILL AND REPRESENTATION, Arthur Schopenhauer. Definitive English translation of Schopenhauer's life work, correcting more than 1,000 errors, omissions in earlier translations. Translated by E. F. J. Payne. Total of 1,269pp. 5⅜ × 8½. 2-vol. set.
Vol. 1: 21761-2 Pa. $10.95
Vol. 2: 21762-0 Pa. $11.95

MAGIC AND MYSTERY IN TIBET, Madame Alexandra David-Neel. Experiences among lamas, magicians, sages, sorcerers, Bonpa wizards. A true psychic discovery. 32 illustrations. 321pp. 5⅜ × 8½. (USO) 22682-4 Pa. $8.95

THE EGYPTIAN BOOK OF THE DEAD, E. A. Wallis Budge. Complete reproduction of Ani's papyrus, finest ever found. Full hieroglyphic text, interlinear transliteration, word-for-word translation, smooth translation. 533pp. 6½ × 9¼.
21866-X Pa. $9.95

MATHEMATICS FOR THE NONMATHEMATICIAN, Morris Kline. Detailed, college-level treatment of mathematics in cultural and historical context, with numerous exercises. Recommended Reading Lists. Tables. Numerous figures. 641pp. 5⅜ × 8½. 24823-2 Pa. $11.95

THEORY OF WING SECTIONS: Including a Summary of Airfoil Data, Ira H. Abbott and A. E. von Doenhoff. Concise compilation of subsonic aerodynamic characteristics of NACA wing sections, plus description of theory. 350pp. of tables. 693pp. 5⅜ × 8½. 60586-8 Pa. $13.95

THE RIME OF THE ANCIENT MARINER, Gustave Doré, S. T. Coleridge. Doré's finest work; 34 plates capture moods, subtleties of poem. Flawless full-size reproductions printed on facing pages with authoritative text of poem. "Beautiful. Simply beautiful."—*Publisher's Weekly.* 77pp. 9¼ × 12. 22305-1 Pa. $5.95

NORTH AMERICAN INDIAN DESIGNS FOR ARTISTS AND CRAFTS-PEOPLE, Eva Wilson. Over 360 authentic copyright-free designs adapted from Navajo blankets, Hopi pottery, Sioux buffalo hides, more. Geometrics, symbolic figures, plant and animal motifs, etc. 128pp. 8⅜ × 11. (EUK) 25341-4 Pa. $7.95

SCULPTURE: Principles and Practice, Louis Slobodkin. Step-by-step approach to clay, plaster, metals, stone; classical and modern. 253 drawings, photos. 255pp. 8⅛ × 11. 22960-2 Pa. $9.95

CATALOG OF DOVER BOOKS

THE INFLUENCE OF SEA POWER UPON HISTORY, 1660–1783, A. T. Mahan. Influential classic of naval history and tactics still used as text in war colleges. First paperback edition. 4 maps. 24 battle plans. 640pp. 5⅜ × 8½.
25509-3 Pa. $12.95

THE STORY OF THE TITANIC AS TOLD BY ITS SURVIVORS, Jack Winocour (ed.). What it was really like. Panic, despair, shocking inefficiency, and a little heroism. More thrilling than any fictional account. 26 illustrations. 320pp. 5⅜ × 8½.
20610-6 Pa. $7.95

FAIRY AND FOLK TALES OF THE IRISH PEASANTRY, William Butler Yeats (ed.). Treasury of 64 tales from the twilight world of Celtic myth and legend: "The Soul Cages," "The Kildare Pooka," "King O'Toole and his Goose," many more. Introduction and Notes by W. B. Yeats. 352pp. 5⅜ × 8½.
26941-8 Pa. $7.95

BUDDHIST MAHAYANA TEXTS, E. B. Cowell and Others (eds.). Superb, accurate translations of basic documents in Mahayana Buddhism, highly important in history of religions. The Buddha-karita of Asvaghosha, Larger Sukhavativyuha, more. 448pp. 5⅜ × 8½. ,
25552-2 Pa. $9.95

ONE TWO THREE . . . INFINITY: Facts and Speculations of Science, George Gamow. Great physicist's fascinating, readable overview of contemporary science: number theory, relativity, fourth dimension, entropy, genes, atomic structure, much more. 128 illustrations. Index. 352pp. 5⅜ × 8½.
25664-2 Pa. $8.95

ENGINEERING IN HISTORY, Richard Shelton Kirby, et al. Broad, nontechnical survey of history's major technological advances: birth of Greek science, industrial revolution, electricity and applied science, 20th-century automation, much more. 181 illustrations. ". . . excellent . . ."—Isis. Bibliography. vii + 530pp. 5⅜ × 8¼.
26412-2 Pa. $14.95

Prices subject to change without notice.

Available at your book dealer or write for free catalog to Dept. GI, Dover Publications, Inc., 31 East 2nd St., Mineola, N.Y. 11501. Dover publishes more than 500 books each year on science, elementary and advanced mathematics, biology, music, art, literary history, social sciences and other areas.